VEGETRONIC

VEGETRONIC

Extreme Vegetable Cooking

ALEXIS GAUTHIER

Photographs by James Lewis

CLARKSON POTTER/PUBLISHERS
NEW YORK

When I started my cooking apprenticeship, I was told that I should know by heart every single classic dish that made up French gastronomy. I was told I should know my Béarnaise from my Hollandaise, that I should know what a brown butter sauce adds to a fillet of sole, that I should be reverential to everything Escoffier had ever said and done.

So I learned it, and without realizing, I became just another recipe follower.

I started to question everything they wanted me to know by heart; why boiling rather than grilling? Why roasted rather than sautéed? Why is vinegar so important in classical French gastronomy? Why fish before meat? I spent many years opening every single door of the French repertoire and found an answer to most of my queries.

There was, however, one question that I could never find a rational answer for . . .

Why did vegetables never get more than a supporting role in the gastronomic world?

There were no answers to be found. It was just a fact.

So for my love of plants, and anything that didn't have a heartbeat, to be enjoyed at the dinner table, I decided to put vegetables in command and create my new green world . . . a "vegetronic" world, where plants would be instrumental to the process of deliciousness.

A world where a crisp, bright, and shiny broccoli, simply roasted with grain mustard and coated in veal jus, will be the star of a dinner party. A world where the flavor and texture of a carrot will be a well of inspiration, and a world where a persimmon will be touched and respected like a first love.

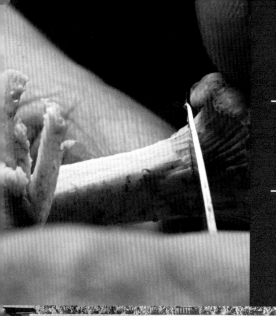

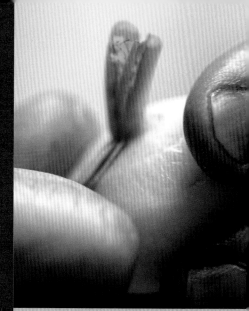

ROMILLY
STREET W1
CITY OF WESTMINSTER

Since the industrial revolution, vegetables have been treated badly. They have been ignored, expelled, segregated, demoted, and abused in every kitchen: top chefs, my mother, my sister, your wife, your son—everyone is guilty.

Vegetables are good for society, but somehow society seems to prefer macho meat or feminine fish.

Vegetables are the maligned minority of the kitchen—only half-accepted if they are happy to go along with the macho star of the dish. They have not yet achieved the level of acceptance that they deserve.

Who wants to leave the exclusivity of vegetables to vegetarians?

NOT ME.

I believe that a vegetable can stand in the kitchen among the top ingredients.

A vegetable has the capacity to be the star of a dish: the central component where it can shine on its own.

Where its great flavor can stand alone or be married to fish or meat flavors, all the while retaining its own personality and being understood for what it is.

Well, I can tell you that vegetables have found a crusader in me.

I can carry the Green Cross and show the world from my kitchen (and this book) that salsify can match the finest filet of beef, or pumpkin the most delicious scallops.

Equality for vegetables!

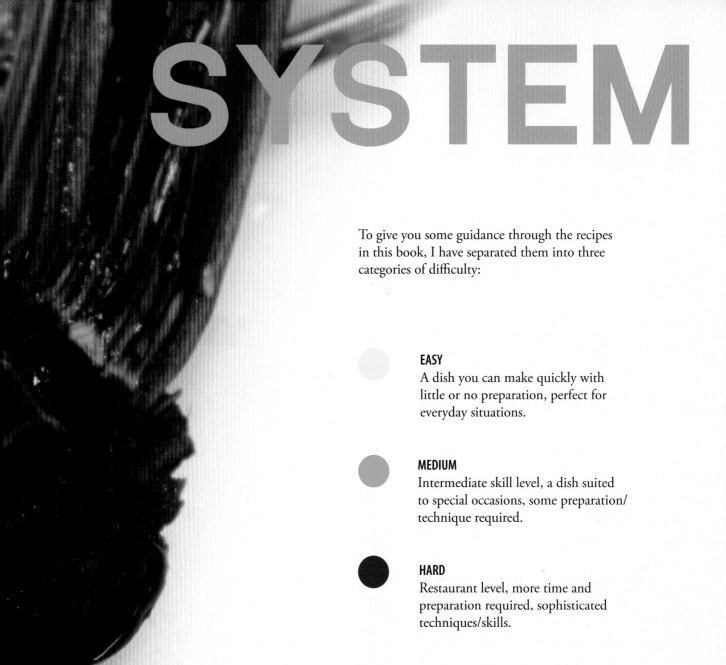

SYSTEM

To give you some guidance through the recipes in this book, I have separated them into three categories of difficulty:

EASY
A dish you can make quickly with little or no preparation, perfect for everyday situations.

MEDIUM
Intermediate skill level, a dish suited to special occasions, some preparation/technique required.

HARD
Restaurant level, more time and preparation required, sophisticated techniques/skills.

All recipes can be completed in a typically equipped kitchen.

RECIPES BY D

1: EASY

2: MEDIUM

FFICULTY

3: HARD

NEW! Get our free iPad app

HARLIE NCENSORED!
Rpwood's Dirtiest Secrets Exposed

ANGIE FREAKS OUT ON BRAD
GET OUT OF MY HOUSE!

BREAKING NEWS!
Star

PAGES OF
HOCKING NEW PHOTOS

GUESS WHO

Stars lose fight with
CELLULITE

GUESS WHO

KATE

HARLIE NCENSORED!
Rpwood's Dirtiest Secrets Exposed

ANGIE FREAKS OUT ON BRAD
GET OUT OF MY HOUSE!

BREAKING NEWS!
Star

PAGES OF
HOCKING NEW PHOTOS

GUESS WHO

Stars lose fight with
CELLULITE

GUESS WHO

KATE

HARLIE NCENSORED!
Rpwood's Dirtiest Secrets Exposed

ANGIE FREAKS OUT ON BRAD
GET OUT OF MY HOUSE!

BREAKING NEWS!
Star

PAGES OF
HOCKING NEW PHOTOS

Stars lose fight with
CELLULIT

GUESS WHO

KATE

GA

NEXT DOO

DIVA

camp

B attitu

ov

THE WAL

Tw

dansk   WONDER

SONGS
OF
MIGRATION

CALORIES

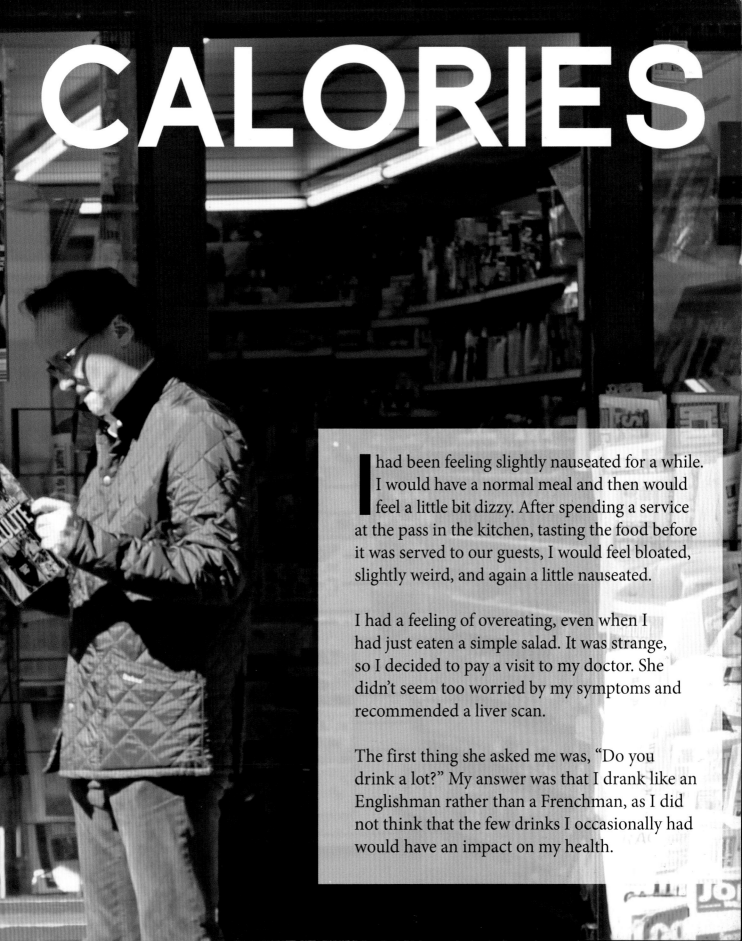

I had been feeling slightly nauseated for a while. I would have a normal meal and then would feel a little bit dizzy. After spending a service at the pass in the kitchen, tasting the food before it was served to our guests, I would feel bloated, slightly weird, and again a little nauseated.

I had a feeling of overeating, even when I had just eaten a simple salad. It was strange, so I decided to pay a visit to my doctor. She didn't seem too worried by my symptoms and recommended a liver scan.

The first thing she asked me was, "Do you drink a lot?" My answer was that I drank like an Englishman rather than a Frenchman, as I did not think that the few drinks I occasionally had would have an impact on my health.

So there I was, lying down in a doctor's room with my tummy covered in weird gel and looking slightly wary. The nurse came and rubbed a small camera over my stomach, and the doctor took some pictures. It took five minutes, and then I was asked to get dressed.

Seriously, I had been overindulging on calories without realizing it. I started to think, Okay, so every night I spoon in 30 bowls of risotto, have 25 slices of cooked meat, about 30 spoons of different meat and fish jus, eight to ten bread rolls, four or five different desserts, a tasting of puff pastries, Chantilly cream, mashed

"Counting calories was the only way to stay alive."

When I saw the specialist who had checked my scan, she was giggling and almost arrogant. "Are you a chef?" she asked. "Yes," I replied, giving her a don't-you-know-who-I-am? kind of look. With a very wide smile she said, "You have a fatty liver. It is time to count. Count your intake of calories. You have been flooding your liver in fat and you are now paying the price for it. The only way out of this is to start counting calories and stick to what you are supposed to eat. No more, no less!"

I was a bit worried and wondered if this was going to be fatal. She looked at me as if I was stupid and said, "A glass of wine is a glass of fat, so good luck." She laughed, then asked me the name of my restaurant (which she had never heard of) and took $500 from my credit card.

potatoes, raviolis with different stuffings, sautéed vegetables, creamy mushrooms, spoons of consommé, creamy soup, browned buttered pieces of fish, glazed vegetables . . . every service, twice a day, six days a week for the past 15 years.

So I reckoned that I had been slowly poisoning myself, while making sure that my guests had perfectly cooked meat, precisely timed risotto, not oversugared whipped cream, etc.

I hadn't even reached 40 years old and my liver was as fat as a French duck ready to be slaughtered. That reminded me I had been tasting our delicious Terrine de Foie Gras for the past 15 years at a rate of ½ ounce per service, twice a day, six days a week, meaning that my body had tried to get rid of just over 5 ounces of foie gras.

That's about 300 fat duck livers!

Not exactly good for me.

Any anti–foie gras campaigner would have been delighted and would call it a fair revenge—unlike my gastroenterologist, who now knew exactly the source of my illness!

Counting calories was the only way to stay alive. So how would I know how to calculate the number of calories I was consuming on a daily basis?

Easy! It took me 10 minutes of research on Google to find out what top athletes do, as a general rule, to ensure they never exceed the right amount of calories.

First of all, I look at labels. By law in the UK, calories have to be published on

It is easy to use and is recommended by athletes. It is so simple that it takes less than 5 minutes per recipe to calculate. I enter the ingredients list with the quantity and the number of portions it is supposed to serve, and I press enter. My four-year-old daughter could work it out.

Then I made a small list of things that I know I should be careful with: a glass of wine, a slice of white or brown bread, a square of dark chocolate, a scoop of sorbet . . .

I did not start going to the gym three times a week, I did not stop drinking wine, and I did not stop eating red meat. However, I have managed to lose 10 percent of my weight in the space of four months.

"I had the information and thought my customers had a right to know the calories in each dish."

supermarket packaging, so it is very easy for me to control my intake when I am at home and using precooked food.

In the kitchen, I use an app called Caloriecount.com.

Now, almost two years down the line, I have not regained my old weight and at my last liver scan, the amount of fat covering my liver was less than half of what it had been.

So when I decided to print calories
on my menu back in spring 2011, I
did not do it out of good conscience.
I had the information and thought
that my customers had a right to know
the number of calories in each dish.
What if someone like me entered my
restaurant and needed to make sure
of his or her calorie intake without
compromising their choice?

There was nothing nannyish in trying
to inform my guests. Just like the price
of an item on the menu, I thought
that it was fair to know the impact a
particular dish may have on the body.

I did not change the way I cooked, nor
did I ever think of removing butter or
cream from some recipes. Our Tasting
Menu was 1,900 calories.

A day's calorie intake!

JUICES

I like to season vegetables with juices. Not to bastardize their aroma and taste, but to balance their flavor. Meat, fish, crustacean, or vegetable juices: I find plenty of inspiration in these. They have become indispensable basic tools over the years for developing my recipes. They feed my imagination, and their combinations are never-ending.

I discovered this when I realized for the first time that I loved the taste of vegetables glazed in meat juice more than the meat itself. Sometimes I just felt like having the vegetables, but not the meat that seemingly must come with it.

This probably comes from my mother and grandmother, who would never wash a baking dish before using it a second time for roasting carrots, tomatoes, and eggplants . . .

There would be eggplant and thyme the day after the leg of lamb, cardoon and bread after roast beef, carrots and salted butter after the loin of veal, and braised endive after a baked sea bass.

But my favorite combination was probably the one my grandma would make a day or two after a roast chicken. She would keep the baking dish in the fridge, and then would stuff some tomatoes with herbs and soaked white bread. She would line the tomatoes on the baking sheet and cook them in the oven until the tomatoes almost exploded! The taste of those tomatoes was unbelievable. They tasted like tomatoes, but also had a meaty flavor because their flavors were enhanced by the juice and fat of the chicken. I could smell it and exactly break down the taste in the oven.

I knew it wasn't tomatoes and chicken cooking together, but tomatoes cooked in chicken juice.

Here are the basic jus, made from natural meat and fish juices, you will need to master if you want to start playing with taste and being creative.

CHICKEN JUS

For 2 cups of ready-to-use jus

Difficulty level: easy
Calories: 100
Preparation time: 3 hours

10 oz. chicken wings

¼ cup olive oil

½ onion (roughly chopped)

½ carrot (roughly chopped)

16 cups water

Cut the chicken wings into equal sizes. Pour the olive oil into a large pan. When the oil is smoking, put in the chicken wings and roast them slowly at a low heat. When they are the same color (golden brown), add the onion and carrot. Roast them well for about 3 minutes.

Then pour in 4 cups of water. Let the water reduce until it is almost dry in the pan, and then add another 4 cups of water and reduce again. Repeat twice more until the juice is dark and the chicken wings have been completely cooked. Strain the jus. You can either keep it in the fridge for up to 4 days or you can freeze it.

When needed, just reheat it in a small pan with a teaspoon of butter.

LAMB JUS

For 2 cups of ready-to-use jus

Difficulty level: easy
Calories: 100
Preparation time: 3 hours

10 oz. not-too-fatty lamb trimmings (shoulder, neck, or leg; ask your butcher, they are usually free)

¼ cup vegetable oil (sunflower is usually best)

4 cloves garlic (crushed using the palm of your hand)

½ onion (roughly chopped)

½ carrot (roughly chopped)

16 cups water

Cut the lamb trimmings into equal sizes (1½ inches x 1½ inches is usually best). Pour the vegetable oil into a large pan, and when the oil is smoking, add the lamb trimmings and roast them slowly at a low heat. Add the garlic cloves and stir without overroasting. When the meat and garlic are of the same light brown color, add the onion and carrot. Roast them as well for about 3 minutes.

Then pour in 4 cups of water. Let the water reduce until almost dry in the pan. Add another 4 cups of water and reduce again. Repeat this once again until the juice is dark and the lamb trimmings are breaking down. Strain the jus. You can either keep it in the fridge for up to 4 days or you can freeze it. You will notice that this juice has quite a fatty consistency. Do not remove the fat as it holds all the flavor.

When needed, just reheat it in small pan with a teaspoon of butter before adding to your vegetables.

BEEF JUS

For 2 cups of ready-to-use jus

Difficulty level: easy
Calories: 100
Preparation time: 3 hours

- 10 oz. beef trimmings (not too fatty)
- ¼ cup olive oil
- ½ onion (roughly chopped)
- ½ carrot (roughly chopped)
- 2 tablespoons unsalted butter
- 16 cups water

Cut the beef into equal pieces. Pour the olive oil into a large pan. When the oil is smoking, put in the trimmings of beef and roast them slowly. When they are golden brown, add the onion and carrot. Roast them as well for about 3 minutes.

Remove the beef, carrot, and onion and drain the pan. Return to the heat and add the butter. Make the butter foam until it almost turns brown (hazelnut) and add the beef, carrot, and onion in, then pour 4 cups of water. Let the water reduce until almost dry in the pan, and then add another 4 cups of water and reduce again. Repeat this until the jus is dark and the beef trimmings are completely soft. Strain the jus. You can either keep this jus in the fridge for up to 4 days or you can freeze it.

When needed, just reheat it in a small pan with a teaspoon of butter before adding to your vegetables.

SHRIMP JUS

For 2 cups of ready-to-use jus

Difficulty level: easy
Calories: 100
Preparation time: 3 hour

- 4 tablespoons olive oil
- 6 oz. shell-on shrimp heads
- ¼ carrot (roughly chopped)
- 2 oz. leek (white part thinly sliced)
- 2 soft tomatoes (roughly chopped)
- 1 teaspoon brown sugar
- ¼ lemon
- 10 basil leaves
- ½ bunch lemongrass
- 16 cups water

Into a large casserole dish, pour the olive oil. When smoking, add the shrimp heads and break them up with another pan or rolling pin. Just think of someone you hate and release your anger. Smash the heads, making sure that the brains have been emptied of their liquid.

Add the carrot, leek, and tomatoes and roast for 3 to 4 minutes. Stir vigorously, and then add the brown sugar, lemon, basil, and lemongrass.

Let everything roast for a couple of minutes, then add the water to cover everything with liquid and cook at a slow simmer for about 2 hours. Then strain the jus and keep in the fridge or freezer.

Just like the meat jus, a shrimp jus will need to be reheated with a small spoonful of butter before serving.

FISH JUS

For 2 cups of ready-to-use jus

Difficulty level: easy
Calories: 100
Preparation time: 3 hours

- 3 tablespoons unsalted butter
- 2 oz. leeks (white part thinly sliced)
- ½ carrot (roughly chopped)
- 1 salmon head
- 3 oz. fish trimmings
- 3 oz. fish bones
- 1 teaspoon brown sugar
- ½ shallot (roughly chopped)
- 1 bunch thyme
- 2 soft tomatoes (roughly chopped)
- 2 tablespoons white wine vinegar
- 2 cups cooking white wine
- 16 cups water

Into a large casserole dish, add the butter. When it starts foaming, add the leek and carrots and stir for 3 minutes. Then add the salmon head, fish trimmings, and bones. Stir vigorously, and add the brown sugar, shallots, thyme, tomatoes, and vinegar. Stir for another 2 minutes.

Add the white wine and reduce to almost dry.

Add the water and cook for 20 minutes at high heat. Strain and reduce for another hour.

There should be 2 cups of fish jus by the end of this process.

Just like the meat jus or shrimp jus, you will need to reheat the jus in a pan with a small quantity of butter before using.

BROTH

CHICKEN BROTH

Makes 2 cups

Difficulty level: easy
Calories: 100
Preparation time: 3 hours

1 large chicken 3½ to 4½ lb. (ask your butcher for a roaster)

Neck, wings & chicken feet

12 cups water

4 large carrots (peeled)

3 turnips (peeled)

2 bunches celery (roughly chopped)

4 leeks (opened, sliced & washed)

2 cloves garlic

1 sprig thyme

1 bay leaf

Pinch salt

1 teaspoon sea salt

1 teaspoon black peppercorns

Into a large cooking pot, put the chicken together with the neck, wings, and feet. Cover with cold water and bring it to a boil.

When it starts boiling, remove from the heat, drain, and rinse the chicken, neck, wings, and feet. It is important to rinse the meat properly to make the broth very clear.

When the meat is well rinsed, put it back in the cooking pot together with the carrots, turnips, celery, leeks, garlic, thyme, bay leaf, and a pinch of salt.

Cover with cold water and bring to a boil. When it starts boiling, reduce the heat, making sure that it simmers very slowly.

Let the broth slowly cook for 4 hours. The broth may produce some gray froth, which is a mixture of blood remaining in the chicken and some dirt from the vegetables. You must remove this foam every hour or so.

Make sure to taste the broth after 4 hours. You may need to let it cook for another 1 or 2 hours. This happens when the chicken you are using does not have a great flavor. However, if you are happy with the taste of the broth, remove it from the heat and add a teaspoon of sea salt and a teaspoon of black peppercorns. Let them infuse while the broth cools down.

Pass the broth through clean cheesecloth to remove all the impurities. Keep the stock in the freezer for up to 4 months or in the fridge for up to 4 days.

FISH BROTH

Makes 4 cups

Difficulty level: easy
Calories: 100
Preparation time: 3 hours

- 1 salmon head
- 4 carrots (peeled & roughly chopped)
- 2 leeks (sliced & chopped)
- 2 bunches celery (roughly chopped)
- 3 shallots (peeled & chopped)
- 1 large onion (cut in 2)
- 1 head garlic (cut in 2)
- 4 cups dry white wine
- 12 cups water
- 1 teaspoon sea salt
- 1 teaspoon black peppercorns
- 6 oz. fish bones (ask your fishmonger; they're usually free)
- 1 bay leaf
- 1 sprig thyme
- 4 cloves (planted in the onion)

Rinse the salmon head. Do not remove the eyes, as Escoffier would have taught me. Salmon eyes are delicious when they are cooked. Trust me.

Wash and rinse all the vegetables. Drain and dry them. It is very important that all vegetables are cleaned, which helps make the broth as clear as possible.

Put a large cooking pot on the heat and pour in the wine, water, sea salt, and black peppercorns. Bring it to a boil and add the remaining ingredients one by one.

Let the broth slowly cook for 2 hours.

Remove from heat and let the broth cool down. Delicately remove the salmon head and remove the eyes. Eat them; they are delicious. Pass the broth through cheesecloth and let it cool.

You can either freeze the broth for up to 4 months or keep it in the fridge for up to 4 days.

VEGETABLE BROTH

Makes 4 cups

Difficulty level: easy
Calories: 100
Preparation time: 3 hours

- 6 carrots
- 4 turnips
- 2 leeks
- 2 bunches celery
- ½ bunch parsley
- ½ bunch chervil
- 8 cups water
- ½ teaspoon sea salt
- ½ teaspoon black peppercorns

Peel, wash, and cut all the vegetables into chunky pieces. Make sure to wash and rinse the parsley and chervil, as they may carry dirt. It is important that all vegetables are perfectly washed to make the broth as clear as possible. Dry the vegetables using a clean cloth and place into a large cooking pot.

Cover with very cold water. The broth always needs to start cooking from very cold. You can even prepare the vegetables the day before and keep them in the fridge in the water they are going to cook in. Bring the pot to boiling point and add the parsley, sea salt, peppercorns, and chervil. Let the broth cook very slowly for 2 hours.

Pass the broth through clean cheesecloth and throw away the vegetables. They will have lost all their taste to the broth, so they are really redundant.

Taste the broth to see if it needs more salt or pepper. This is the last opportunity to rectify the seasoning while it cools down. It will keep in the fridge for up to 4 days or in the freezer for 4 months.

I love drinking this broth on its own, but one of the great ways to appreciate it is to reheat it and break an egg into it. Leave to cook for 3 minutes and serve. It will be the best poached egg you will ever have.

FLOWERS

When I was young, I used to love deep-fried acacia, crêpes made with rose blossom water, a salad of in-flower dandelion and chive blossoms, and desserts made with mimosa blossoms.

My grandmother, Albertine, was a real genius with flowers. She used them everywhere: salads, stuffings, desserts, and in a lot of her favorite wines and nonalcoholic drinks.

She never used a cookbook in her life, preferring to develop her own recipes. She loved gardening and eating. She thought the two went hand in hand. She was right, and her cooking became more and more floral over the years. She never tried to instruct me with her cooking. She never tried to convince me that she knew better than anyone else. Everything was natural for her and so long as it tasted good to her, it was fit to be served.

I thought that, as a typical Provençal grandmother, she would have found enough satisfaction from cooking fruits and vegetables. I was so wrong! She was the queen of flowers and herbs!

While studying my family history, I realized we had a connection with North Africa and Italy, two places where they have been using flowers in cooking for generations. It must have been in her genes!

In the northern region of Liguria, Italy, people have been using flowers as stuffing for meat, tarts, and even fish for hundreds of years. Mixed with potatoes, for example, flowers bring a touch of seasonality. In Mexico, hibiscus or cactus are used in recipes dating back to the Aztec era.

& HERBS

In the Balkans, North Africa, and the Middle East, flowers have been used for centuries, mainly for adding individual aromas to traditional recipes. Classic combinations like Ras el Hanout, herb-flavored couscous, rose-petal marmalade, rose jelly, or rose syrup are common there.

Flowers have long been used in Southeast Asia, too. Pink lotus is prepared with rice wine in Laos, and camellia leaves are served deep-fried or cooked like green vegetables in Indonesia. Japanese cooks use plum and peach flowers to make some fantastic and healthy infusions and to make delicious wine. Camellia is also a key ingredient in a celebratory meal for any person reaching the age of 90. Recipes using chrysanthemum leaves for steamed dumplings and stuffed crab or fish are also common throughout the region.

Easy to grow and to look after, flowers can be a great source of inspiration. Most flowers are edible. You can add a touch of exotic flavor with just a few edible plants grown in your garden or on your balcony.

DAYLILY RISOTTO

Difficulty level: medium
Calories: 350
Preparation time: 40 minutes

Daylilies are easy to grow and are attractive ornamental plants. They are also one of the tastiest plants in my garden. This plant can tolerate heavy clay and shady space. I particularly like the young leaves when they are not too fibrous. You can serve them in salad with a few drops of reduced Italian red wine (Vino Cotto), salt, pepper, and olive oil. You can also dry the leaves to make a paste to use as a soup thickener.

Serves 4

- 2 cups daylily blossoms (blanched & chopped to an almost pastelike texture)
- 2 cups daylily foliage (quickly deep-fried in oil)
- 3 tablespoons salted butter
- 1½ oz. shallots (peeled & finely chopped)
- 5 oz. long-grain brown rice
- ½ teaspoon tamarind powder
- 4 teaspoons freshly grated ginger
- ½ cup dry white wine
- 8 cups water
- 1¼ cups olive oil
- 5 oz. baby squid (cleaned & thinly sliced)
- 1 lime (juiced)
- Salt & pepper
- 1½ oz. sliced almonds

When the daylily leaves are a little bit older, you can pan-fry and serve them like spinach. You will be amazed by their salsify taste! They actually sometimes taste more like salsify than salsify. I recently heard some people argue that they taste like creamed onion.

Either way, it is a very special ingredient. The other good thing with this lily is that you can actually eat the root freshly grated in salad or rubbed against meat before cooking it. It tastes amazing!

Prepare the daylily blossoms and foliage.

In a large, thick-bottomed pan, melt a teaspoon of butter, then add the shallots. Stir until the shallots get hot and shiny.

Cook slowly for 2 minutes and add the rice. Stir continuously while making sure that neither the rice nor the shallots turn brown.

Add the daylily paste, tamarind powder, and fresh ginger and stir. Add the white wine and allow it to bubble and reduce for 3 to 4 minutes. Then start adding the water ladle by ladle for 18 minutes while continuously stirring. Add ¾ cup of olive oil at the end and divide between 4 soup plates.

In a separate pan, quickly fry the baby squid in smoking oil until they start releasing water. Drain and put them back in the pan with a spoon of butter, the juice of one lime, salt, pepper, and the almonds.

Add the squid and almonds on top of the rice. Add the foliage of a few deep-fried daylilies on top of each plate and serve.

CHRYSAN

THEMUM

O n November 1 each year France celebrates the dead. All Saint's Day is a day of remembrance for families who have lost loved ones and also a day of joy and celebration for florists across the country.

It is a day when millions of overpriced chrysanthemums are brought to adorn tombs for the delight of . . . um . . . well, no one really! I always wondered what the point was of spending a fortune on some really ugly plants that absolutely no one would ever thank you for.

So if you are thinking only about your own pleasure, you must transform these plants into something useful, hence the following recipe for burned wine.

If you feel bad about it, you can always buy some dried chrysanthemum leaves from any good Asian food market.

FLOWER WINES

I have been living in the UK for many years now, but something I still admire is the constant need to find a good excuse for alcohol consumption: celebrations, business meetings, friend gatherings, sporting events, end of the week, weekends . . . Anything is a reason to indulge. Well, now I have just created another one: gardening. You will never again come across as an obsessed alcoholic, but rather like a sophisticated gardener who can transform plants into alcohol. Brilliant.

CHRYSANTHEMUM BURNED WINE *(Pictured)*

Difficulty level: easy
Calories (per glass): 213
Preparation time: 2 hours 30 minutes

Serves 6

4 cups dry red wine (750 ml)

2 handfuls dry chrysanthemum leaves

2 oranges (peel)

1 bay leaf

½ cinnamon stick

½ vanilla bean

Boil the red wine for 5 minutes and add the dried chrysanthemum leaves. Boil for another 5 minutes and remove from the heat. Let the leaves infuse for 1 hour.

Pass the liquid through clean cheesecloth and put back in a clean pan. Add the remaining ingredients and boil for 5 minutes.

Let it infuse for another hour.

Filter once again and reheat just before serving.

SAGE WINE

Difficulty level: easy
Calories (per glass): 229
Preparation time: 2 months

For 1 bottle

10 dried sage leaves

1 bunch dried thyme

1 tablespoon honey

1 bottle white wine (750 ml)

Chop the dried sage and thyme leaves and mix them with the honey. Add the white wine and mix until the leaves look mushy.

Let it macerate for 12 hours. In order to get the full taste of the sage, you will need to stir the maceration every hour.

Strain through clean cheesecloth and bottle it.

Keep for 2 months before drinking.

FLOWER WINES

DANDELION WINE

Difficulty level: easy
Calories (per glass): 213
Preparation time: 2 months

Serves 4

10 cups water

4 handfuls dandelion flowers (or wild pissenlit), equivalent to 5 oz.

1 teaspoon grated ginger

1 orange (peel)

1 lemon (peel)

2¼ lb. superfine sugar

1 teaspoon dry yeast

¾ cup dry white wine

Boil the water and wait until it has cooled down (about 10 minutes).

Clean the flowers after removing the stems. Cover them with the boiled water and let them macerate overnight.

Add the ginger and the orange and lemon peels, bring to a boil, and let them cook for 30 minutes. Filter through cheesecloth and then add the sugar.

Add the dry yeast with the wine. Cover the pan with a clean dish towel and put a lid over it. Let the wine ferment for 2 days at room temperature.

Leave the wine to rest in the bottle for at least 2 months before drinking.

ROSE WINE *(Pictured)*

Difficulty level: easy
Calories (per glass): 213
Preparation time: 1 month

Serves 6

6 oz. dry rose petals

1 tablespoon honey

1 bottle dry white wine (such as a good-value white Côtes du Rhône)

Before the end of summer, dry some rose petals, preferably from the most powerful plant. Mash the petals with honey and mix them with the wine.

Let the mixture macerate for 12 hours in a bowl covered with a clean dish towel at room temperature. Filter through a clean cheesecloth. The rose wine may look a little cloudy at this stage, but you don't worry—this will settle during the resting time.

Keep in the bottle for one month minimum and drink very cold.

This wine is perfect with roasted nuts or preserved fruits.

FUCHSIA

The fuchsia is a great little shrub for the shady part of your garden. It produces little flowers all through the summer, which are followed by tasty small fruits. Everyone at home loves these little fruits, especially my neighbor's cat, who has been helping himself. One day the cat is going to pay for that! I just wonder what he might taste like—would his meat be very fuchsia-ish?

FUCHSIA-TOFU-GINGER MIX *(Pictured)*

Difficulty level: medium
Calories: 95
Preparation time: 30 minutes

Serves 4

3 oz. fuchsia berries

3 oz. fuchsia fruits

2 tablespoons honey

2 tablespoons olive oil

2 tablespoons soy sauce

2 teaspoons pickled ginger

10 oz. firm tofu

4 teaspoons pink shallots

2 scallions

Pepper

1 tablespoon bonito flakes

This is the best way to eat the fuchsia (not the cat).

In a bowl, mix the berries together with the fruits.

Add 1 tablespoon of honey, 1 tablespoon of olive oil, and 1 tablespoon of soy sauce. Add the chopped pickled ginger and keep at room temperature.

Slice the tofu block into ⅛-inch-thick slices and line them on a serving tray. Chop the shallot and scallion and sprinkle over the tofu. Add a bit of black pepper. Pour on the remaining honey, soy sauce, and olive oil.

Pour the mix of fuchsia over it and add some bonito before serving.

Serve cold.

LATE-SUMMER TOMATO & FUCHSIA SALAD

Difficulty level: easy
Calories: 80
Preparation time: 15 minutes

Serves 4

4 large Roma tomatoes (with a shiny dark red color)

2 cloves garlic (peeled & roughly chopped)

3 oz. mix of fresh fuchsia leaves & flowers

⅔ cup good-quality olive oil

Salt

Fat Italian tomatoes in summer paired with fuchsia are a perfect match. You must prepare them a little in advance, and once they have both released their delicious juices, you will want to dip back into it again and again. . . .

Clean the tomatoes and pat dry. Cut them into thick slices of about ¼ inch and put them in a large bowl. In a different bowl, crush the garlic with the fuchsia leaves. When the fuchsia-garlic mix reaches a paste consistency, add olive oil and salt. Pour the dressing on top of the tomatoes and add the fuchsia flowers.

JASMINE-SCENTED HYDROMEL

Difficulty level: easy
Calories (per glass): 280
Preparation time: 10 minutes Fermentation time: 20 days Rest time: 2 months

This is a fermented honey wine drink that is as old as human civilization. I've added jasmine and rose petals. When you drink it you feel as if the gods themselves have just entered the party and you can smell their perfume.

For 4–5 750ml bottles

- 12 cups water
- 10 oz. honey
- 3 handfuls strongly scented dry rose petals
- 1 handful jasmine leaves
- 1 egg
- 1 cup Muscat wine

Boil the water in a large pan and add half of the honey. Let it boil for 3 minutes, then add the rose petals, jasmine leaves, and the egg. Whisk for 3 minutes, then remove from the heat. Let the stock infuse for 1 hour. Then cover it with a clean dish towel and leave it at room temperature for 20 days.

By this time, it will have fermented. Filter the stock through a clean cheesecloth and add the Muscat wine.

Store in tightly sealed bottles and leave to rest for a minimum of 2 months.

Note: You should always use untreated rose and jasmine petals, preferably from your garden, never sprayed with pesticides. If you don't have one, make sure to buy your petals from a reputable source.

LEMON BALM

My garden is full of lemon balm from the end of March until early July, when the leaves become too large and less intensely flavored. They have a slightly peppery, lemony taste. I love them in salads when teamed with lobster and crunchy vegetables. I also love lemon balm infusion, which tastes a bit like lemony spinach—strange, yet very pleasing and a lot more interesting than mint infusion, for example.

LEMON BALM, PEAR & OYSTER *(Pictured)*

Difficulty level: hard
Calories: 60
Preparation time: 30 minutes

Serves 4

¾ cup dry white wine

2 cups water

12 oysters (open & rinsed)

2 Bartlett pears (thinly sliced & kept in lemony water)

5 oz. fresh lemon balm leaves (½ blanched & thinly chopped)

¾ oz. shallots (peeled & thinly sliced)

¼ cup heavy cream

Kosher salt and pepper

In a pan, bring the wine and water to a boil. Add the oysters and leave for 2 minutes. Refresh them in ice and keep them on a clean cloth to gently dry.

Place the slices of pear on a clean, flat surface. On each slice, spread a spoonful of thinly chopped lemon balm leaves topped with a few thin slices of shallot. Place an oyster on each one.

Roll them up like small cannelloni and wrap a fresh lemon balm leaf around each one. Top each with a little heavy cream, rock salt, and black pepper.

Difficulty level: easy
Calories: 0
Preparation time: 5 minutes

LEMON BALM INFUSION

Serves 1

Handful lemon balm

Hot water

Take a handful of freshly picked and washed leaves with a bit of stem still attached. Then pour some almost boiling water over and let it infuse for 5 minutes. Drink while still hot.

Lemon balm is so plentiful in my garden that I provide the restaurant with its annual stock for free.

Belfast
manufacture)
IRISH
Dun Laoghaire
(Kingstown)
Wicklow
ST. GEORGE'S CHANNEL
neat)
Cardigan
Milfo
wanse
(Coa
Ilfracomb
Tin-
CORNWALL
Devo
rpool to South America
West Africa

LOVAGE BLOODY MARY

Difficulty level: easy
Calories: 140
Preparation time: 10 minutes

Lovage is very easy to grow in full sun or in a light shade position. I covered my side garden wall with lovage. It grew so much that it blocked the sun from the black tomato I was so proud of. After harvesting the leaves I remove the plant from my garden—it is too invasive. Lovage has an interesting taste. When cooked, it is a bit like bitter celery. It is nice to add a few lovage leaves when preparing a green stuffing.

Serves 1

¼ cup vodka

½ cup tomato juice

¾ oz. lovage leaves (quickly blasted in a food processor)

1 teaspoon lemon juice

4 dashes Worcestershire sauce

4 drops Tabasco sauce

Pinch celery salt

Pinch black pepper

Lovage's peppery flavor is always a nice addition. However, as it is such a powerful herb I always suggest using it with caution. It can be extremely overpowering.

Try a Bloody Mary with the lovage juice and it will be the best you've ever had.

Combine, shake, and strain all of the ingredients.

Serve over ice.

Celery and tomato heaven.

LOVAGE & PEPPERMINT BUBBLEGUM

Difficulty level: hard
Calories: 20
Preparation time: 30 minutes

I have managed to crack the bubblegum mystery. As a child, I would dream of being able to make sweets to impress my friends. My proudest moment would have been to create magical BUBBLEGUM, the only sweet that could be shaped and would last for hours. Finally I have mastered the art of bubblegum making. I don't dream of synthetic flavor anymore. Now it's real peppermint for freshness and lovage for punch. A child's nightmare but an adult's heaven . . .

Serves 1

- ½ bunch peppermint
- 20 lovage leaves
- 4 teaspoons corn syrup
- 1 tablespoon gum base (available for purchase online)
- 1 teaspoon liquid chlorophyll (available for purchase online)
- 4 teaspoons confectioners' sugar
- 2 tablespoons cornstarch

Blend the peppermint and lovage with the corn syrup until you get a very liquid syrup. It's okay if there are still a few bits inside. Place it in the fridge.

Make sure the gum base is at room temperature. Put it in a bowl and start softening it with the palm of your hand. When it starts to soften, put the bowl either in a microwave oven at full power for 30 seconds or in a conventional oven for 5 minutes at 350°F.

Add the peppermint syrup and the chlorophyll. Continue mixing the gum with your hand.

Add half of the confectioners' sugar and continue pressing the gum with your hand.

On a clean surface, sprinkle some cornstarch and continue pressing and folding the gum base in with the cornstarch until it starts getting really soft.

Add the remaining confectioners' sugar and continue flattening the gum.

When the gum is easy to flatten, cut some shapes and sprinkle them with cornstarch so they don't stick together.

You can keep the gum for up to 2 weeks in an airtight container.

MARSHMALLOW & RICOTTA RAVIOLI

Difficulty level: medium
Calories: 412.25
Preparation time: 45 minutes

This easily grown plant likes both dry and moist soil and requires a sunny position. The leaves are perfect for stuffing when mixed with ricotta. Everyone asks me where I found this amazing spinach. It is tender and soft, retaining its green color like no other green leaves when cooked. Just perfect!

Serves 4

Stuffing

- 2 cups marshmallow leaves (can be purchased online)
- 6 oz. leeks
- ¼ cup extra-virgin olive oil
- 2 tablespoons ricotta cheese
- 2 eggs
- Salt & pepper
- 4 teaspoons grated Parmesan cheese

Pasta

- 1½ cups flour
- 2 eggs
- 1 tablespoon water
- 1 teaspoon white wine vinegar
- Pinch salt

For Serving

- Extra-virgin olive oil
- Grated Parmesan cheese
- Black pepper

Making the stuffing

Wash and roughly chop the marshmallow leaves.

Wash and slice the leeks.

Heat a little olive oil in a pan. Add the chopped leeks, salt, and water. Cover and cook for 3 minutes. Add the marshmallow leaves and cook for another 3 minutes. Drain and chop very finely.

Put the chopped ingredients in a big bowl then add the ricotta, eggs, and pepper and mix together. Taste and season again. This stuffing should be very peppery (I like it like that). Add a bit of olive oil and grated Parmesan cheese.

Making the pasta

You can either buy some ready-made dumpling wrappers from your local Chinatown market (delicious) or use the following recipe.

Mix everything in a bowl with your hands. Once you have a smooth even dough, cover with plastic wrap and let it rest for at least 1 hour in the fridge.

Roll out the dough very thinly (good luck if you don't have a pasta machine) and cut it into circles of 2 inches x 2 inches.

In each little circle of pasta, place one spoonful of stuffing and cover with another piece of pasta. Seal the borders by gently pressing on them.

Boil some water in a saucepan with a bit of salt. Throw in your stuffed pasta and wait until the pasta comes back to the surface of the boiling water. Wait another 30 seconds and remove them.

Serve on a plate with plenty of olive oil, grated Parmesan cheese, and black pepper. This recipe makes about 20 ravioli.

MIMOSA

The fluffy little flowers in late winter and early spring are edible. They make great sweets when served at the end of the meal to accompany coffee or tea. They are also a perfect snack during the day, just deep-fried and tossed in confectioners' sugar.

CRISPY MIMOSA FLOWER

Serves 4

Difficulty level: easy
Calories: 95
Preparation time: 15 minutes

10 oz. mimosa flowers

½ cup superfine sugar

¼ cup water

¼ cup vegetable oil

1 teaspoon confectioners' sugar

Dry the flowers for 3 weeks after harvesting.

In a pan, put the superfine sugar together with the water. On a very high heat, bring it to a caramel-like color, then remove the pan and throw in the mimosa, together with the vegetable oil.

Stir vigorously and remove from the pan, transferring onto an oiled baking sheet. Let the flowers cool down, then roughly chop with a knife into small pieces when fully cooled. Sprinkle with confectioners' sugar and serve.

CHOCOLATE & MIMOSA MOUSSE

Serves 4

Difficulty level: medium
Calories: 380
Preparation time: 40 minutes

6 oz. dark chocolate (70% cocoa minimum)

¾ cup heavy cream

1 handful dried mimosa flowers

2 teaspoons confectioners' sugar

In a thick-bottomed pan, pour the dark chocolate and melt it at a very low heat. Make sure to stir the chocolate once melted to dissolve any thick pieces.

In a bowl, whip the cream until it's on the verge of stiff.

Once the chocolate has melted, slowly pour it into the cream and continue whipping until the mix is blended well together. Fill 4 short glasses with the cream and store in the fridge for at least 20 minutes before serving.

Just before serving, sprinkle the dried mimosa flowers over the chocolate mousse.

Add a bit of confectioners' sugar and serve.

CORSICAN MINT

Broccoli & cauliflower fake risotto

Difficulty level: easy
Calories: 207
Preparation time: 30 minutes

Corsican mint is a very delicate and low-growing plant that likes a shady position in your garden. It is also the perfect mint for salad. You will notice that the taste is not overly strong but will last a long time. The infusion made from it is very good for your health, especially when you have a cold.

Serves 4

½ cup extra-virgin olive oil

3 tablespoons shallots (finely chopped)

¼ cup dry white wine

6 oz. heads broccoli (cut into small ¼ in. x ¼ in. cubes)

6 oz. cauliflower (broken into small pieces)

Salt & pepper

1½ cups water

¾ oz. mascarpone

3 tablespoons grated Parmesan cheese

2 oz. freshly picked tiny Corsican mint leaves

In a large pan on low heat, pour 2 tablespoons of olive oil and stir in the shallots. Slowly cook for 3 minutes, until the shallots look brilliant and soft. Add the white wine and reduce for 2 minutes.

Then add the broccoli, cauliflower, and a pinch of salt. Stir gently, making sure you don't break the pieces of broccoli. Add the water and continue stirring with a spoon for 3 minutes.

Add the mascarpone and stir until it has dissolved completely in the mix. Let it boil for 2 minutes and add the Parmesan cheese and the remaining oil, stirring constantly.

When the mix seems amalgamated, add the mint and pepper and serve quickly.

Everyone will think that you have made a very light broccoli and mint risotto, not realizing that the rice texture is actually from the cauliflower!

ROSE-PETAL SORBET

Difficulty level: medium
Calories: 280
Preparation time: 4 hours

Rose petals are not very often used in traditional French cuisine. Too feminine, too delicate. Not an ingredient Escoffier would have ever dreamed of being associated with. I discovered so many fantastic ingredients the day I decided to move away from classical French training. Realizing that rose petals were more than something that looked good in a bouquet was seriously life-changing!

Serves 8

2 cups sugar

2¼ cups water

⅔ cup rosewater

½ vanilla bean (cut in 2)

Zest of 3 lemons

½ oz. rose petals (untreated)

1½ cups Champagne

4 teaspoons pomegranate syrup

4 small packets Pop Rocks candy (optional)

In a heavy-bottomed saucepan, bring to a boil the sugar, water, rosewater, vanilla bean, and lemon zest.

Add the rose petals and let them infuse.

Pass through a cheesecloth and chill.

Add the Champagne and churn in an ice cream machine.

Scoop into bowls. Drizzle pomegranate syrup over and sprinkle on some Pop Rocks, if using, just before serving.

VIOLET

Violet is such a fantastic little flower. It can really be a chef's best partner. It is so versatile and can be used in syrups, essences, jellies, creams, or cakes. Early May is the best time to remove violet leaves from the stems. Dry them out for two weeks. This will leave you enough time to decide what to do with them.

VIOLET & FENNEL SOUP *(Pictured)*

Difficulty level: easy
Calories: 120
Preparation time: 45 minutes

Serves 8

¼ cup extra-virgin olive oil

3 large fennel bulbs, thinly sliced

1 baking potato (peeled & roughly chopped)

Pinch fleur de sel (or smoked salt if you can find some)

6 cups water

2 handfuls violet leaves (as fresh as possible)

Pepper

Into a large pan, pour a splash of olive oil. When the oil is smoking, put in the sliced fennel and the potato together.

Stir and add the salt. Add the water and 1 handful of violet leaves. Cover and allow to cook slowly.

After half an hour, pass through a blender and add the last handful of violets.

Serve when hot with a pinch of freshly ground black pepper.

VIOLET GRANITA

Difficulty level: medium
Calories: 110
Preparation time: 3 hours

Serves 4

8 cups water

2 cups sugar

2 handfuls dry violet flowers

In a pan, pour the water and the sugar. When boiling, add the violet leaves, remove from the heat and let them infuse until it has cooled down.

Place the mixture in a bowl and put in the freezer.

Every 2 hours, take it out and scratch it with a fork so it turns into the texture of a granita.

Serve in frozen glasses topped with some fresh petals.

VIOLET JELLY

Difficulty level: medium
Calories: 188
Preparation time: 2 hours

This recipe reminds me of my grandmother, who used to feed me jelly for breakfast on toasted bread with salted butter. She had a great collection of jellies! The flavor she gave me would depend on the weather, her mood, or simply what was left in the cupboard, but my favorite was her violet jelly.

Serves 10

2¼ lb. Golden Delicious apples

2¼ lb. superfine sugar

¼ cup water

½ lemon (juiced)

6 oz. dried violet leaves

Peel the apples and rinse them with hot water. Put them in a large pan and cover with water. When boiling, remove from the pan (they should be soft by then) and break them into pieces.

Into a large pan, put the sugar and the hot water. Cook on a low heat and when the sugar is almost turning brown, add the broken apples and stir for 15 minutes on a very low heat. Add the lemon juice and the violet flowers, remove from the heat, and leave to cool.

When the jelly has cooled down, stir again and pour into jars.

I love it when there are a lot of chunky pieces of apples left in the jelly.

The taste of the violet becomes so strong within the apples that it's almost like they've slept together!

OR, HOW DO YOU USE VEGETABLES AS A NATURAL DIVERSIFIER?

Sensibility plays a big role when it comes to treating a vegetable. The more responsive you are, the more likely you are to find that a vegetable is the perfect tool to express yourself via cooking.

First, open your eyes and look at where you are. Where do you stand? What time of the year is it? What do you want? What does your body need? Have you ever wondered what surrounds you and if there is anything that has a parallel life to yours?

Be aware of your senses and use the seasons as a guideline; this will naturally bring natural diversity. Everything will start feeling so normal. Yet so inspiring!

You'll surprise yourself by growing excited to be able to buy the first asparagus in the spring. It will remind you that winter is now gone for good and the season has already started to show its fantastic produce.

You'll be sad to be using those delicious summer squashes for the last time this year, but will be happy to know that the pumpkins are already showing great promise for the coming autumn.

That is the amazing life of vegetables and you must live at their pace. Not too fast or too slow.

They go on and on following the months. By giving you a sense of time, they also make you feel part of the season.

They make you feel part of it all.

They make you feel alive!

COOK

ABLES

Vegetables, dry or fresh, are an immense source of inspiration for me. I actually think they are the bases of my "alimentation": I think of them as a starter, main course, or even dessert.

Vegetables are very often sidelined by chefs and cookbooks. They are in danger of becoming the exclusive property of vegetarians. And I don't want that. Vegetables are for all of us.

We tend to think that vegetables are just there to be good for you. We have been told that we should eat spinach on a regular basis in order to get enough iron, folic acid, and potassium. And, by the way, it also regulates blood pressure, boosts the immune system, and has anticancer properties. So let's order a side dish of spinach. It doesn't matter if it tastes good or not. It's good for me. So should I care if it tastes good?

Yes, of course you should care. There are so many ways to cook vegetables: boiled, grilled, roasted, simmered, braised . . .

And there are so many ways to season them: salt, pepper, meat juices, fish juices, vinegar reduction . . .

I actually think you can be a lot more creative with vegetables than with meat or fish. You can play with their textures, their shapes, and their smells in ways impossible with meat or fish. And if you use vegetables as they come into season, you will naturally change your diet and bring more excitement to your meals.

That is the amazing life of vegetables. They follow the months, giving a sense of time passing. They also make you feel alive. Yes, you are alive!

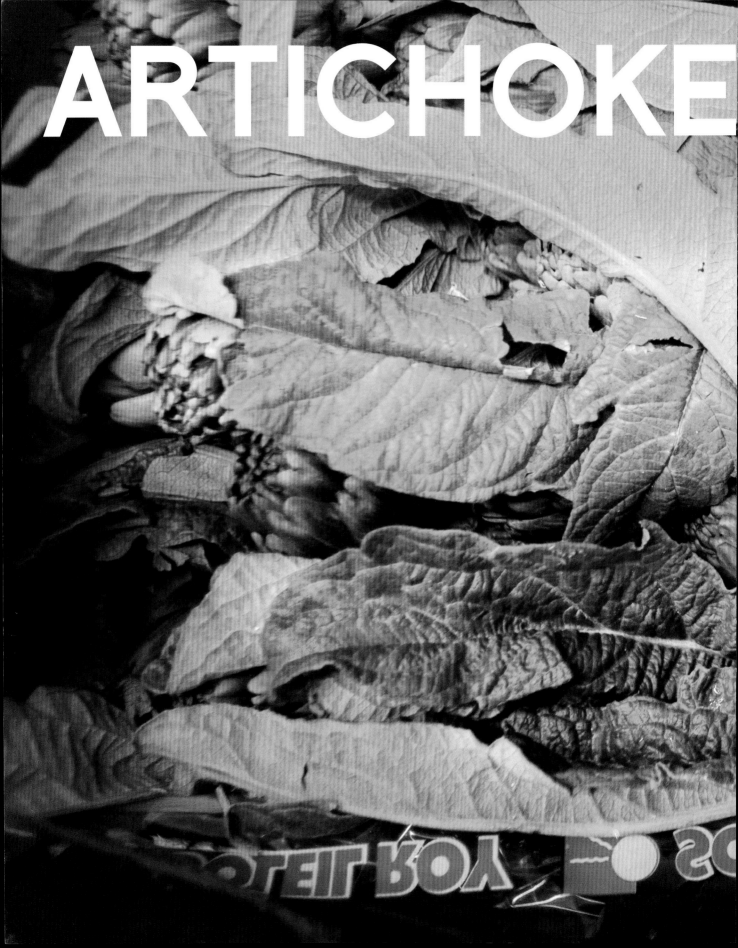

ARTICHOKE

ARTICHOKE "BARIGOULE"

Difficulty level: hard
Calories: 150
Preparation time: 45 minutes

This dish was my worst nightmare as a child. It looked ugly and tasted weird, and its texture was so off-putting that I would probably have preferred eating haggis. I just couldn't understand how my parents could find any pleasure in having this dish other than enjoying seeing me suffer. I guess getting old is a bit weird: you tend to enjoy things that you would have detested in your youth—so alongside hairy chests and Thatcher's rhetoric, Artichoke "Barigoule" is something that I now really like.

Serves 4

- **1 shallot**
- **1 carrot**
- **8 button mushrooms**
- **2 oz. smoked bacon**
- **16 small purple artichokes**
- **2 tablespoons extra-virgin olive oil**
- **Salt & pepper**
- **2 sage leaves**
- **5 oz. white wine**
- **8 large slices Parma ham**
- **1 tablespoon unsalted butter**
- **1¼ cups chicken broth**

Cut the shallot, carrot, mushrooms, and bacon into small cubes.

Remove the outside leaves of the artichokes. Go around them with a very sharp knife to get rid of any green skin that is left.

Remove the hairy inside of the artichokes and put the artichokes in very cold water.

Pour a bit of olive oil into a hot pan. When it starts smoking, add the carrots, shallots, and salt.

Stir, making sure it doesn't brown. When the carrots and shallots are shiny, add the mushrooms and bacon. Continue stirring for an extra minute and add the sage leaves and half the wine.

Let the liquid evaporate, and strain.

Stuff each artichoke with the chopped mix of vegetables and wrap them in half a slice of Parma ham.

Place the artichokes in a sauté pan and add the butter, chicken broth, and the remainder of the wine.

Cover and cook for 20 minutes. Serve on a large plate with a pinch of pepper.

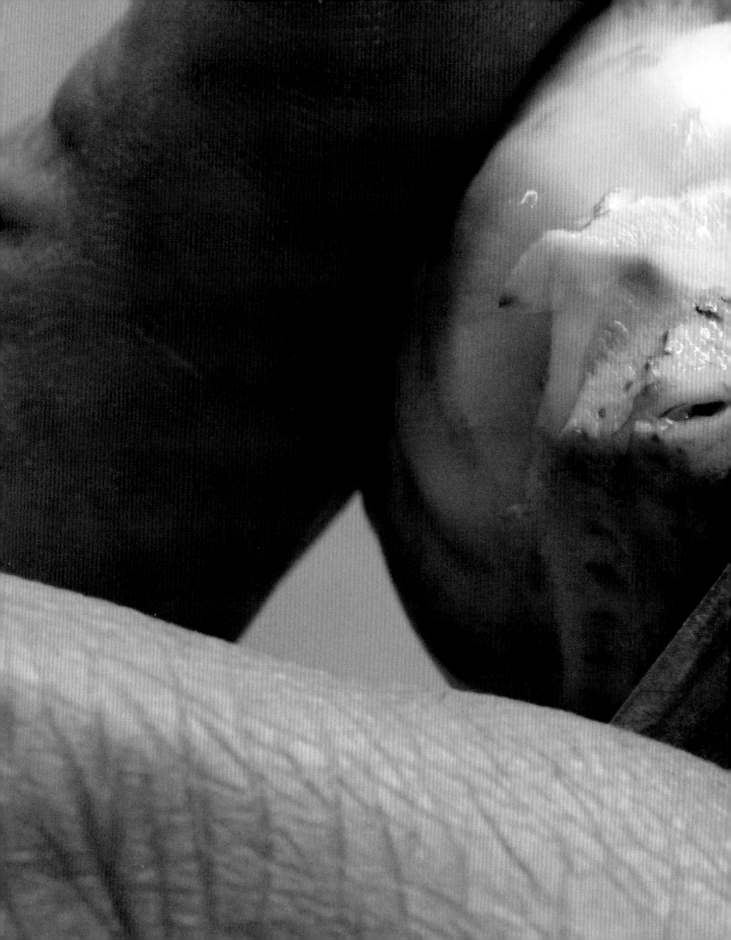

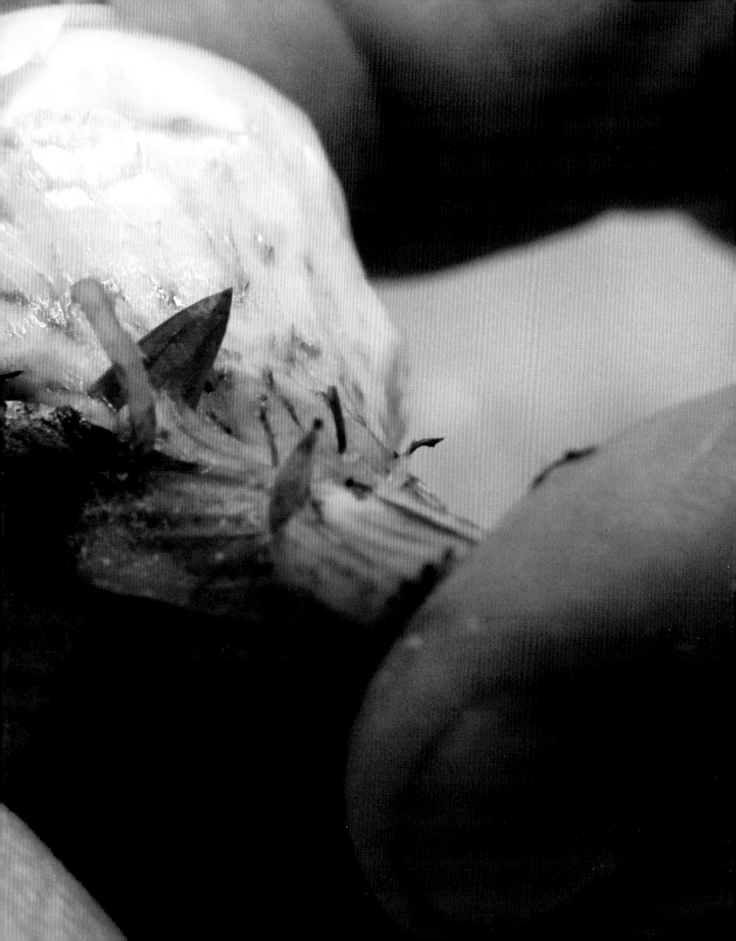

JERUSALEM ARTICHOKE & CHERVIL SOUP

Difficulty level: medium
Calories: 220
Preparation time: 30 minutes

The Jerusalem artichoke is one of the easiest vegetables to cook and also one of the tastiest. A winter or spring vegetable, it is of the same family as potatoes but its taste is as delicate as an artichoke. Very rich in phosphorous and potassium, very filling as well: 100g of Jerusalem artichokes equals 80 calories! The good thing with this vegetable is that you can't perform miracles with it. I mean you cannot transform its shape, for example. You cannot transform its taste or its texture. It is a simple and real vegetable and I love it like that.

Serves 4

- 2¼ lbs. Jerusalem artichokes
- 1 oz. butter
- Salt & pepper
- 1¼ cups low-fat milk
- 1 bunch chervil
- ½ cup water

The Jerusalem artichoke never had the same success as the potato or the artichoke and even now is still struggling to get stocked in supermarkets. I have always wondered why.

Peel and chop the Jerusalem artichokes and keep them in icy-cold water.

Place the butter in a hot pan. When it turns brown, add the Jerusalem artichokes and sauté with salt.

As soon as they are slightly colored, add the milk and cover with a tight lid. Cook at low heat for 6 minutes.

After that, pour the contents of the pan into a blender and mix until you have a uniform and beige liquid cream.

Clean the food blender and blend the bunch of chervil, reserving a few leaves for decoration, with the water, salt, and pepper.

Reheat the Jerusalem artichoke soup and serve in hot soup cups. Pour the chervil mixture over the soup and serve with more chervil leaves on top.

JERUSALEM ARTICHOKE & CRISPY CHICKEN SKIN

Difficulty level: hard
Calories: 288
Preparation time: 1 hour

Is there a better dressed vegetable dish than this one? A mushy vegetable is the real star. If it was on its own, it would be deadly boring. The moment you add a little bit of texture (crispiness from the chicken), a depth of flavor (brown butter and Parmesan cheese), and the deliciousness of slightly fat meat jus, it is not naked anymore. It shines and takes on another dimension.

Serves 4

- **3 oz. chicken skin (your butcher will usually give it away)**
- **Salt & pepper**
- **10 oz. Jerusalem artichokes**
- **½ cup extra-virgin olive oil**
- **2 tablespoons unsalted butter**
- **2.5 oz. grated Parmesan cheese**
- **½ cup chicken jus**

On a clean surface, flatten the chicken skins and season them with salt and pepper. In a very hot nonstick pan, fry each piece until it turns crisp (usually 4 minutes on each side). Rest on a grill. When cold and hard, cut into triangle shapes.

Peel the Jerusalem artichokes and make sure that you don't leave any skin on. Put in cold water until you cook them to retain their bright white color.

Drain the artichokes. In a large pan pour the olive oil. Add half of the butter to the pan and wait until it turns brown. Add the Jerusalem artichokes and roast them slowly on a low heat, then add salt and put a lid on. Check frequently. The artichokes should release enough water during the cooking process that transforms into steam so they won't burn.

After 4 minutes, the Jerusalem artichokes are cooked and are still in their original shape. At this moment, bring the heat very high to evaporate any water left in the pan.

Add the remaining butter and let it brown. Shake the pan, making sure not to smash the artichokes. When the butter has browned, sprinkle over the grated Parmesan cheese and remove from the heat.

Serve on 4 small plates and place the triangles of chicken skin over the artichokes.

Reheat a little chicken jus in a pan and pour onto each plate.

ASPARAGUS

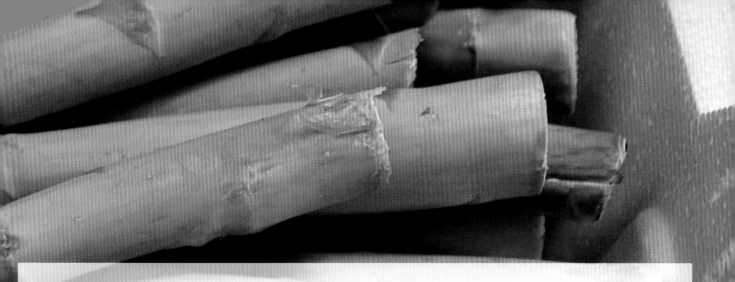

W hether green, white, purple, or wild, asparagus has been popular for centuries.

The ancient Greeks thought asparagus was an aphrodisiac, and Louis XIV of France wanted to have it on his table every day starting in December. The first unsustainable king. His family paid for it later!

We now know that asparagus is rich in potassium, folic acid, vitamins C and K . . . And I know from my grandmother that it is also good for the kidneys.

Asparagus season begins in March and finishes in June. You should not be tempted to eat asparagus before or after. White, green, or purple, asparagus has to be very fresh if you want to eat it at its best (usually 2 days after it has been harvested).

Fresh asparagus should be slightly wet at its base and firm yet easy to break. A soft asparagus has lost its taste, but we knew that already—not only with asparagus.

The best way to cook asparagus is to pan-fry it in order to stabilize its chlorophyll. This technique will always end up producing green and shiny asparagus that, most important, will not turn dark and will never taste boiled and washed out.

GREEN ASPARAGUS

Lemon confit, poached quails' eggs & Parmesan crisps

Difficulty level: hard
Calories: 224
Preparation time: 1 hour

Serves 4

Asparagus
- 1 bunch green asparagus
- Salted water

Poached quails' eggs
- ¼ cup water
- 2 tablespoons white wine vinegar
- Salt
- 12 quails' eggs

Lemon confit
- 2 lemons
- 4 teaspoons granulated sugar
- 2 tablespoons white wine vinegar

Parmesan crisps
- 3 oz. finely grated Parmesan cheese
- 1 teaspoon all-purpose flour

Sauce
- ½ cup balsamic vinegar
- ½ cup red wine
- 1 tablespoon unsalted butter

For the asparagus

Remove the hardest part at its base, about a fifth of the asparagus, depending on its freshness. (The fresher the asparagus, the longer the softer part will be.) Peel the asparagus halfway, removing the little spikes, and boil them for 5 minutes in salted water. As soon as they are cooked, place in cold water and drain once cold.

For the poached quails' eggs

Boil the water with the vinegar and salt. Break the eggs into boiling water for 2 minutes, then place them in cold water.

Making the lemon confit

Peel the lemons. Slice the peel into equal strips. Melt the sugar and vinegar in a pan. Add the juice and skins of the two lemons. Cook at a very low heat until the strips of lemon look opaque and the liquid has evaporated.

Making the Parmesan crisps

Mix the Parmesan cheese with the flour and pass it through a sieve, making sure that only the finest particles are kept. In a nonstick pan, on a low heat, sprinkle the mix, making round shapes. Remove once they have melted without letting them brown.

Making the sauce

Into a small pan, add all the ingredients. At low heat, reduce until the liquid has evaporated by half.

Serving the dish

Reheat the asparagus in a pan with a little bit of butter, salt, and pepper. Place the lemon confit and asparagus on the plate. Add the quails' eggs and Parmesan crisps. Pour the sauce around and over.

WARM SALAD OF GREEN ASPARAGUS
Gnocchi of ricotta & crunchy bacon

Difficulty level: hard
Calories: 250
Preparation time: 1 hour

Serves 4

Asparagus

> 6 oz. green asparagus
>
> 8 slices bacon (chopped)

Dressing

> ½ cup port
>
> 1 teaspoon brown sugar
>
> ½ cup extra-virgin olive oil
>
> 2 tablespoons white wine vinegar
>
> 1 tablespoon unsalted butter

Gnocchi of ricotta

> 4 oz. ricotta cheese
>
> ½ tablespoon flour
>
> 1 tablespoon grated Parmesan cheese
>
> 1 egg
>
> Salt & pepper

Serving

> ½ cup water
>
> 2 tablespoons unsalted butter
>
> 2 tablespoons grated Parmesan cheese
>
> Pepper

For the asparagus

Remove the hardest part at its base, about a fifth of the asparagus, depending on its freshness. (The fresher the asparagus, the longer the softer part will be.) Remove every little spike around it. Slice lengthways very thinly with a Japanese mandoline (or a very sharp knife if you haven't got one) and keep in icy water so the slices become crunchy and slightly bent.

Bake the bacon at 425°F for 10 minutes or until the bacon is crispy but not burned. Alternatively, you can pan-fry the bacon until it turns golden.

Making the dressing

In a pan, pour the port together with the brown sugar, oil, and vinegar. Reduce to half of its original volume and add the butter.

The reduction will turn thick once the liquid absorbs butter. Remove from the heat and keep at room temperature until serving.

Making the gnocchi of ricotta

Mix all the ingredients in a food processor until they turn into a smooth paste. Season with salt and pepper and put in the freezer for 20 minutes.

Once the ricotta mix is cold, form some small quenelles with two coffee spoons and poach them in boiling water for 3 minutes. Remove from the water and keep them covered in plastic wrap until serving.

Serving the dish

Reheat the gnocchi in a pan with the water, butter, and 2 tablespoons Parmesan.

Meanwhile, in a medium bowl, toss the asparagus with half of the dressing. Add salt and pepper. Place the gnocchi on the plate and cover them with the asparagus. Add the bacon and pour the remains of the dressing around it.

Add some freshly ground pepper and serve.

MEDLEY OF WHITE ASPARAGUS
Chives & crispy chicken skin

Difficulty level: medium
Calories: 125
Preparation time: 45 minutes

When I think of a vegetable as the "star" of a dish, I need to balance its entire composition. White asparagus, despite its refinements, needs a lot of help. As a general rule, add crunch if soft, add sweet if bitter, add green if white, add animal if vegetable.

Serves 4

Asparagus

1 lb. 2 oz. (1 bunch) white asparagus

1 small bunch chives

Chicken skins

3 oz. chicken skin (your butcher will usually give it away)

3 tablespoons unsalted butter

Salt & pepper

Serving

½ stick (4 tablespoons) unsalted butter

¾ oz. ground almonds

10 tablespoons chicken jus (page 29)

For the asparagus

Cut off the hardest part of the asparagus.

Peel from top to bottom, making sure not to remove too much of the flesh. Cook the asparagus for 4 minutes in boiling salted water. Rinse under cold running water.

For the chicken skins

Flatten the chicken skins on a clean surface and score them slightly with a knife without cutting them too much. Season them with butter, salt, and pepper.

Sandwich them between two baking sheets and cook in the oven at 350°F for 10 minutes.

Serving the dish

Just before serving, heat the butter in a large pan. When it starts turning brown, add the asparagus and toss until they start to turn golden. Add the chives for another minute, until they are just wilted. Sprinkle the ground almonds into the pan and toss to coat. Remove the asparagus and place it on a plate.

Reheat the chicken jus and pour it around the asparagus.

Add the crispy chicken skins and chives on top of the asparagus.

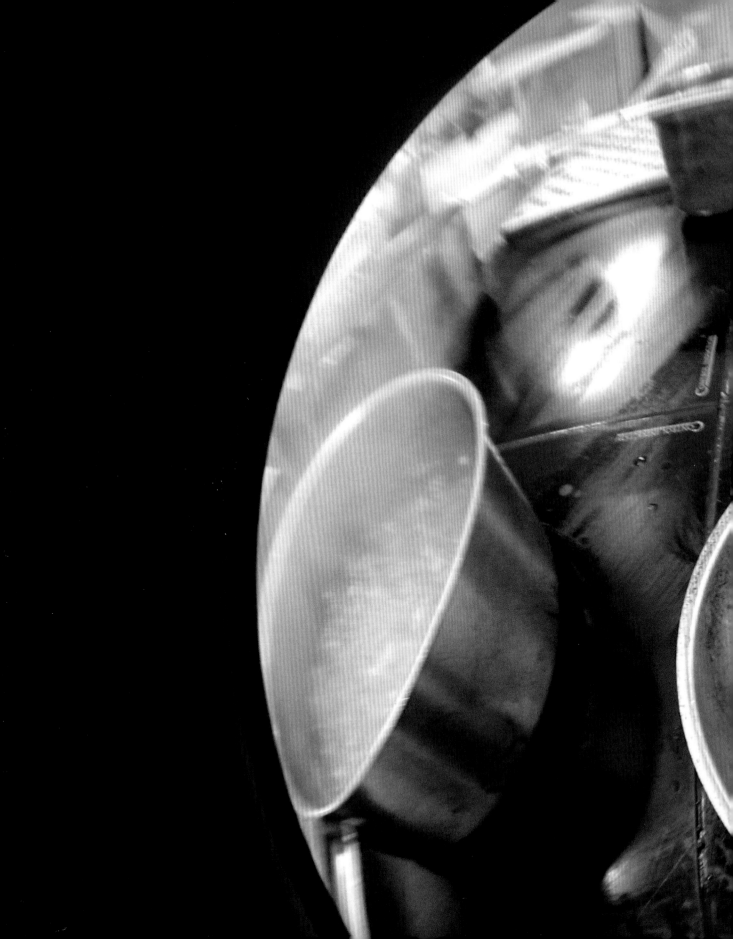

WHITE BEAN SOUP

Peppered, with crunchy lettuce, flat-leaf parsley, red wine & garlic bread

Difficulty level: medium
Calories: 158
Preparation time: 2 hours

The white bean is usually a summer vegetable, but it can also be purchased dry and cooked throughout the year. I like the texture of the white bean, especially when puréed and when mixed with olive oil, herbs, and salt. It becomes like a light mayonnaise. It is also so good for you: it removes excess cholesterol and cleans your digestive tract, and is rich in protein.

Serves 4

- 3 oz. dry beans (borlotti, cannellini, or white)
- About 8 cups water
- ½ onion
- 1 carrot
- ½ leek
- 1 bay leaf
- Salt & pepper
- 2 slices rustic French bread
- 2 cloves garlic
- 1 romaine lettuce
- 1 large bunch flat-leaf parsley (roughly chopped)
- ¾ cup very dry red wine

Place the white beans in a large pot and cover with water. Bring to a boil, drain.

Run the beans under cold water and put them back in the pan. Cover with water and add the onion, carrot, leek, and bay leaf. (Yes, you only need one bay leaf.) Cook very slowly and make sure that there is plenty of water in order for the beans to "swim." The beans tend to double in size while cooking!

You know the beans are cooked when they just melt with a little bit of pressure between your teeth. When you reach this point, you'll realize we have not added any salt. Salt would have broken their thin skin during cooking.

Remove the pan from the heat and add a pinch of sea salt and allow it to infuse in the beans while they cool in the liquid.

Taste again and add more salt if you feel like it. (Always salt with sea salt; otherwise, if you oversalt this dish you won't be able to rectify the mistake. The best is Fleur de Sel de Guérande or de Camargue, but the price is far too expensive for this dish.)

Blend the beans with their cooking stock and slowly reheat them.

Meanwhile, toast the bread and rub the garlic cloves against them. Cut into chunky cubes.

Wash the lettuce and separate the crunchy leaves from the stalk.

Serve in large soup bowls. Place the parsley in the middle of the bowl, top with the bean soup, then the crunchy leaves and the bread. Pour a bit of red wine over each plate and add some black pepper.

HOT SUMMER WHITE BEAN SOUP

Difficulty level: medium
Calories: 245
Preparation time: 2 hours

Growing up in Provence I ate a lot of cold food during the hot summers. Refreshing melon, cold eggplant stews, and salads of sweet and bright tomatoes. There was, however, an exception in our summer food. I really looked forward to enjoying this hot soup in summer. It was served steaming hot, and I remember being so impatient to eat it that I burned my tongue on the first spoonful. The hot combination of white beans, basil, Parmesan cheese, and thyme is still vivid in my mind. No other food reminds me more of my summers in Avignon.

Serves 4

- 10 oz. white beans
- ½ leek (white part only, roughly chopped)
- 1 carrot (roughly chopped)
- 1 onion (roughly chopped)
- 1 bay leaf
- 2 garlic cloves (thinly sliced)
- 10 sprigs dry thyme
- 1 bunch basil
- 10 cups water
- 1 zucchini (roughly chopped)
- 1 overripe tomato (chopped into cubes)
- 8 spring onions (thickly chopped)
- 1 tablespoon sea salt
- 3 oz. rigatoni pasta (cooked, refreshed & chopped)
- 1 tablespoon soy sauce
- 2½ oz. grated Parmesan cheese

Rinse the dried white beans under cold water for 1 minute. Put them in a large cooking pot with the leek, carrot, onion, bay leaf, garlic, thyme, and half of the basil bunch. Cover with the water and cook slowly for 15 minutes.

Add the zucchini, tomato, and spring onions. Cook for another 10 minutes.

Remove from the stove and add sea salt. Stir in the salt gently while making sure not to mush the ingredients.

Let the pot cool.

When you are ready to serve, reheat the beans to the boiling point and add the pasta to the pot along with the soy sauce.

Serve in a hot soup plate with grated Parmesan cheese and the rest of the basil leaves, chopped.

BEET FANTASIA

Crunchy apple, fresh goats' cheese & thyme

Difficulty level: hard
Calories: 180
Preparation time: 1 hour

Back at school, it seemed that at every lunch I was served beet salad as a starter. It was always heavily dressed, and the mustard was far too powerful for the delicate taste of the beet. On top of that, I was always afraid of turning my tongue and teeth entirely red. Now beets are very much à la mode. There isn't a trendy restaurant in London that doesn't celebrate the pseudo-new life of this forgotten (at least for them) vegetable.

Serves 4

- **¼ cup extra-virgin olive oil, plus more for dressing**
- **2 bunches fresh beets (peeled with 1-inch stem attached)**
- **Kosher salt & pepper**
- **8 cups water**
- **2 tablespoons balsamic vinegar**
- **4 oz. fresh goat cheese**
- **4 small bunches fresh thyme**
- **2 Royal Gala apples (thinly sliced)**

Beets are now served in every way and in every form. Raw, half cooked, honey-glazed, grilled, as dessert, and I have even seen the beet featured as a pizza topping! (I have tried it and I can assure you that it tastes as it reads: disgusting.)

Beets are not an easy vegetable to marry. They have such a sweet and powerful flavor that you usually need something acidic and oily to balance the rich taste.

Pour 2 tablespoons olive oil into a hot pan. Once the oil is smoking, add the beets and sauté them until they get very shiny and slightly brown. Add some salt and 4 cups of water. Cover with a lid and cook at a slow simmer for at least 15 minutes. (Check that the water has not totally evaporated after 10 minutes. You may need to add another cup of water depending on how tight the lid is on the pan.) Slice into the biggest beet with a small knife. If it goes in and out without resistance, the beets are cooked.

Add the remaining olive oil and the vinegar to the beet jus in the pan. Stir and let the beet jus, oil, and vinegar come together and form a split dressing. Remove from the heat and let cool.

In a medium bowl, break up the fresh goat cheese with a fork. Add a tablespoon of olive oil, some salt, black pepper, and fresh thyme. Serve the beets warm with a spoonful of goat cheese.

Add the slices of raw apple and serve.

UPSIDE-DOWN BORSCHT

Difficulty level: hard
Calories: 264
Preparation time: 3 hours

Serves 4

Soup

¼ cup vegetable oil

10 chicken wings (cut in 2)

5 oz. beef (cut into cubes)

Salt

1 bunch fennel seeds

½ bunch fresh marjoram

½ white onion (diced)

½ cup red wine

4 cups chicken broth (see page 32)

3 raw beets (grated)

Garnish

3 tablespoons unsalted butter

2 leeks (cleaned & shredded)

1 stalk celery (thinly sliced)

1 medium onion (peeled & diced)

6 Savoy cabbage leaves (boiled & cut into small triangles)

6 oz. beets (you can use vacuum-packed precooked beets cut into small cubes)

Salt & pepper

3 tablespoons sour cream

Making the soup

In a sauté pan with a little oil, pan-fry the chicken wings with the pieces of beef until they are golden brown but not burned.

Add a pinch of salt, the fennel seeds, marjoram, onion, and the wine. Reduce until the mixture is almost dry. Add the chicken broth and the grated beets. Cook at very low heat for 2 hours.

Remove the beef from the broth and thinly slice it. Divide into 4 portions and place the slices at the bottom of soup plates.

Making the garnish

In a sauté pan, melt the butter and add the leeks, celery, and onion. Slowly heat while stirring. Add the savoy cabbage (keeping a little for a garnish), beets, salt, and pepper. Stir constantly while the vegetables slowly continue to heat. Taste and add more salt and pepper if desired.

Spoon the vegetables on top of the slices of beef in the plates and serve the beets and chicken broth on top.

Serve with sour cream on the side and garnish with some savoy cabbage.

COLD SUMMER CREAM OF BROCCOLI & GINGER

Difficulty level: easy
Calories: 85
Preparation time (including chilling): 3 hours 30 minutes

Broccoli is a great way to start the day. You can drink the juice by cleaning it and putting the heads in your juicer. When it is mixed with fresh orange pulp, it is the perfect juice: not too sweet, not too bitter, and with more than just the orange bits!

Or you can try this simple recipe.

Serves 4

- 1 large broccoli head (about 10 oz.)
- 2 tablespoons extra-virgin olive oil
- 1½ oz. onion (peeled & chopped)
- 1 clove garlic (crushed)
- Salt
- 1½ oz. ginger (peeled & grated)
- 2 cups water
- Zest from 1 lime

Clean the broccoli under cold running water. Into a big pot, pour some olive oil. When it starts to smoke, add the broccoli, onion, and garlic.

Add salt and grated ginger. Stir (making sure that nothing browns) and add the water. Cover and wait 10 minutes.

Make sure that the broccoli is tender, then put everything in a blender and blend until everything is creamy and smooth. You may have to add a little water to get the perfect consistency.

Keep in the fridge for a minimum of 3 hours before serving.

Serve with a big splash of olive oil on the top of each glass and some freshly grated lime zest.

WHOLE BROCCOLI

Grain mustard & crunchy radishes

Difficulty level: medium
Calories: 110
Preparation time: 30 minutes

Broccoli is one of the most nutritious vegetables, known for its anticancer properties and antioxidants. It's also antiviral and full of calcium and vitamins. The problem is that, in terms of cooking it doesn't leave much to the imagination. You can't play with its shape and you can't really play with the way you cook it. During the '80s, chefs thought that because of its shape, broccoli would look good in the presentation of dishes. It was the '80s equivalent of microleaves—you saw it everywhere and it looked awful.

Serves 4

1 head broccoli

¼ cup extra-virgin olive oil

1 tablespoon grain mustard

1 egg yolk

1 tablespoon balsamic vinegar

½ bunch long radishes (thinly sliced & kept on ice)

¾ oz. daikon radishes (thinly sliced & kept on ice)

Salt & pepper

½ cup chicken jus (page 29)

It is very rare to find broccoli as the main part of a dish in a restaurant or in a cookbook. But, as with many '80s trends, it is bound to make a comeback very soon, so let's start by putting broccoli as a centerpiece back on the menu.

Choose broccoli whose dark green color is turning purple.

Wash under running water and dry it with a clean dish towel. Cut off the stems at the base of the head.

In a large pan, heat some olive oil and add the broccoli. Pan-fry until it's almost brown, then add a little water and cover for 5 minutes. When the broccoli is almost cooked (you will know when you can insert a knife without resistance), let the remaining water in the pan evaporate.

Prepare the dressing by whisking the grain mustard, egg yolk, the remaining olive oil, and the balsamic vinegar together until the mixture thickens a little. Season to taste with salt and pepper.

Lay all the radishes at the bottom of the plate. Place the broccoli head over them and cover with the dressing.

Pour the hot chicken jus over the broccoli and serve it whole at the table.

BRUSSELS SPROUT LEAVES

Difficulty level: medium
Calories: 170
Preparation time: 45 minutes

Bacon, chestnuts & chicken livers

The first time I told my grandfather that I had decided to move to London to work, he said, "Why are you going there? It is where people eat Brussels sprouts! You can't make anything good with Brussels sprouts." He was referring to a common belief in France that the British only eat gray-boiled Brussels sprouts at every meal to complement two kinds of potatoes. The French also still believe that only they know what is good and how it can be cooked. The barbaric one is always the other one.

Serves 4

14 oz. Brussels sprouts

½ cup extra-virgin olive oil

2 oz. carrot (diced)

2 oz. white onion (diced)

4 slices bacon (thinly sliced)

Salt

2½ oz. vacuum-packed chestnuts

3 tablespoons unsalted butter

4 oz. chicken livers

¼ cup white wine vinegar

¾ cup beef jus (page 30)

I fell in love with Brussels sprouts the minute Mark Birley, the famous founder of Annabel's and Mark's Club, gave me this recipe. It was a classic garnish that his clubs used to serve during the sprout season, and I can assure you that I am now a firm believer that the sprout is a very classy vegetable!

After washing them under cold running water, take one sprout at a time and remove as many outer leaves as you can, making sure to retain only the bright green ones. Dispose of any stained or yellowed leaves.

Despite their size, a good Brussels sprout always has tough, very green leaves. The leaves usually require 10 minutes of cooking in salted boiling water to tenderize them.

Once they have boiled, refresh them under cold water.

In a small pan, heat the olive oil until almost smoking and add the carrot, onion, and bacon. Lower the heat and stir, making sure not to brown. After a couple of minutes the carrots and onion will start looking more and more shiny. Add the Brussels sprout leaves and stir for another minute. Add some salt, then the chestnuts. Cover and cook at medium heat for 5 minutes.

In small pan, heat the butter until it turns brown. Add the chicken livers and sauté them at high heat. Add salt and cook them for a further 2 minutes, continually shaking the pan. Add the vinegar and cook for another 30 seconds. Remove the pan from the heat and place the contents of the pan on a plate.

Reheat the beef jus and serve the Brussels sprouts leaves in soup plates topped with the chestnuts, chicken livers, and the beef jus.

CABBAGE

Cabbage is not to everyone's taste, but there are so many varieties that if you look closely, you'll find one that appeals to you.

My fear had always been eating in a Chinese restaurant and having to smell boiled cabbage for the entire meal. There is something off-putting about it, but when I started to look beyond its smell, I found cabbage to be a very versatile and complex vegetable.

The cabbage is a winter vegetable and is considered a perfect food when it comes to healthy eating. Consumed raw, it detoxifies the stomach and colon, improves digestion, stimulates the immune system, kills bacteria, and is an antioxidant.

CARAMELIZED SAVOY CABBAGE *Liver wrap*

Difficulty level: medium
Calories: 186
Preparation time: 45 minutes

Always buy savoy cabbage when the leaves are very green. The leaves are perfect as a wrap or just roasted in brown butter with lard. Choose the heaviest one you can find, and make sure its leaves are very tight.

Serves 4

1 savoy cabbage

1 bunch romaine lettuce

3 tablespoons unsalted butter

5 cloves garlic (peeled & finely chopped)

1½ oz. onion (peeled & finely chopped)

Salt

¼ cup extra-virgin olive oil

4 oz. chicken livers

¼ cup sherry vinegar

1½ oz. foie gras

Soy sauce

Remove all of the dirty leaves from the cabbage. Cut the base and pull off all the greenest leaves. Put the leaves on top of one another on your cutting board and cut them into thick slices of similar size.

Prepare the romaine by removing the leaves from the stalk, then wash and keep them in the fridge.

In a large pot, put some butter on a low heat. When it starts foaming, add the garlic and onion and cook them until they turn slightly brown. Add the shredded cabbage, salt, and water. Cover and cook for 40 minutes.

Put some olive oil in a sauté pan. When it starts smoking, add the chicken livers and sauté them for 3 minutes. Add a teaspoon of butter and let it turn brown. Deglaze the pan with a dash of vinegar and stir. Remove from the pan and let the livers cool down a little.

Chop the foie gras roughly and place on top of the lettuce leaves. Add the cooked cabbage and chicken livers and serve with a dash of soy sauce.

RED CABBAGE

Always buy red cabbage when it is dark red turning light purple. Do not go for one whose leaves are starting to turn black or with leaves that seem too thin.

SALAD OF RED CABBAGE, DANDELION GREENS & CHICKEN JUS DRESSING *(Pictured)*

Difficulty level: easy
Calories: 75
Preparation time: 1 hour 30 minutes

Serves 4

- ½ red cabbage
- 2 bunches bitter dandelion greens
- ½ bunch flat-leaf parsley
- 4 tablespoons extra-virgin olive oil
- 2 tablepoons balsamic vinegar
- Salt & pepper
- ¼ cup chicken jus (page 29)

Cut the red cabbage thinly and rinse under cold water.

Put the shredded red cabbage in a bowl filled with ice and water and let it become crunchier for 10 minutes in the fridge.

Meanwhile, wash the dandelion greens and parsley.

Put the olive oil, vinegar, salt, and pepper into a bowl. Add the drained red cabbage, dandelion greens, and parsley. Mix and put on plates.

Add a bit of chicken jus to each plate and serve with black pepper.

BRAISED RED CABBAGE, CINNAMON, RED WINE & PORK BELLY

Difficulty level: medium
Calories: 330
Preparation time: 1 hour 45 minutes

Serves 4

- 1 whole red cabbage
- 5 oz. pork belly
- 1 tablespoon sea salt
- ½ onion
- 1 Golden Delicious apple (peeled & chopped)
- 2 tablespoons cinnamon
- 2 tablespoons brown sugar
- ¼ cup cooking red wine
- 1 tablespoon chicken fat (your butcher may have some on hand)
- Salt & pepper

Preheat your oven to 325°F.

Cut the red cabbage thinly and rinse it under cold water. Put it in the fridge for 10 minutes to make it crunchier.

Fill a pot with cold water and add the pork belly and a tablespoon of sea salt. Bring to the boil, drain, and rinse the pork belly under cold water. Cut the belly into small cubes of ¼ inch x ¼ inch.

In a deep pan, put the onion, red cabbage, pork belly, apple, cinnamon, brown sugar, red wine, chicken fat, salt, and pepper. Stir, cover, and cook in the oven for 1 hour.

Serve straight from the oven.

CARDOON

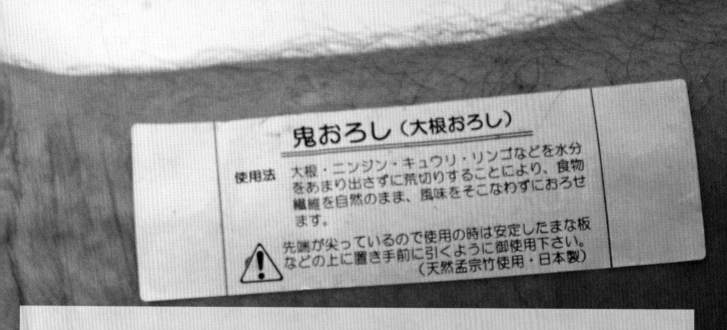

鬼おろし（大根おろし）

使用法　大根・ニンジン・キュウリ・リンゴなどを水分をあまり出さずに荒切りすることにより、食物繊維を自然のまま、風味をそこなわずにおろせます。

⚠ 先端が尖っているので使用の時は安定したまな板などの上に置き手前に引くように御使用下さい。
（天然孟宗竹使用・日本製）

Cardoon was famously used by the Greeks and the Romans. It was grown widely at that time and regarded as a real delicacy.

Cardoon is now something of a second-class vegetable, especially in western Europe. I was surprised to find that most of my customers didn't know it.

My mother used to make a gratin of cardoon for Christmas. She cooked the cardoon with veal marrow, butter, and olive oil. It was very tender and, obviously, incredibly rich!

In traditional French gastronomy, according to Escoffier, cardoons should be cooked in boiling salted water with a lemon cut in half. I don't have to tell you that this is absolutely the wrong way to eat cardoons and I was shocked to find out that nobody wondered if there was any other way to enjoy them.

Until I worked in Ducasse's kitchen. I discovered while there that it could be cooked to a 3-Michelin-star standard.

The way we cooked cardoons was almost the same way as my mother did, except that we took a lot more care than she did to peel them. You have to use the sharpest knife in the kitchen. Cardoons are made of thin fibers that are almost invisible. If you are not careful, you may think that every layer of skin has been removed, but as soon as it is cooked, the unpeeled layers of skin turn black.

I can tell you that I had hours of bollocking and psychological bullying while at Ducasse. The head chef would find it very exciting to stand next to me as my cardoons were cooking. The moment one turned black, he would destroy me in front of all of my colleagues, and repeat again and again that I should quit being a chef and turn to hairdressing instead!

I hated him.

My love for cardoons, however, has never diminished.

CARDOON

MELTING CARDOON GRATIN WITH PARMESAN) *(Pictured)*

Difficulty level: medium
Calories: 230
Preparation time: 1 hour

Serves 4

1 cardoon head

¼ cup extra-virgin olive oil

¾ stick (6 tablespoons) unsalted butter

Salt & pepper

3 cups water

½ cup beef jus

¼ cup grated Parmesan cheese

Peel the cardoons and keep them in cold water. Into a large pan, pour a bit of olive oil and when hot, fry the cardoons, making sure they don't brown. Add the butter together with salt and pepper. Then add some water and cover.

Cook on a very low heat and simmer. Every 3 to 4 minutes, try to put a knife through the cardoon. When there is no resistance, remove the pan from the heat and let it cool.

Put the cardoons in a gratin dish and cover them with their reduced cooking stock, the beef jus, and some freshly grated Parmesan cheese. Put in a very hot oven (425°F) for 3 to 5 minutes.

Serve with a lot of pepper.

RAW CARDOONS WITH ANCHOVY SAUCE

Difficulty level: easy
Calories: 95
Preparation time: 30 minutes

Serves 6

1 cardoon head

40 small anchovy fillets

4 cloves garlic

2 boiled eggs

Salt & pepper

2 tablespoons red wine vinegar

1¼ cup extra-virgin olive oil

Peel the cardoons and put them in very cold water. Store in the fridge for 20 minutes, then drain.

With a mortar and pestle, mix together the anchovy fillets, the garlic, boiled eggs, salt, and pepper until you get a thick paste. Add the vinegar and olive oil. Taste and salt as needed, depending on how salted the anchovies are.

Serve the anchovy paste in a bowl with the crunchy cardoons on the side.

CARROT

Carrots are the most consumed root vegetable in the world. In a traditional French kitchen, the carrot is used almost everywhere. It brings sweetness to sauce and broth, adds texture to cream and velouté, and, most important, shines on its own when it carries a dish.

Carrots are the real star of the vegetable world.

CARROT

HONEYED CARROTS WITH SHRIMP & CUMIN *(Pictured)*

Difficulty level: medium
Calories: 150
Preparation time: 45 minutes

Serves 4

6 oz. carrots

1½ oz. leeks (white part only)

¼ cup extra-virgin olive oil

2 tablespoons honey

1 teaspoon cumin

Salt & pepper

4 shrimp (shell-on, heads on, opened in 2)

2 tablespoons unsalted butter

¼ cup shrimp jus (page 31)

Slice the carrots and the leeks (the same size).

Into a pan, pour some olive oil. When it starts to smoke, toss in the carrots and leeks. When the carrots and the leeks are starting to shine, pour in enough water to cover them. Add a bit of honey and cumin and cover with a lid for 2 minutes. Then remove the lid and let the water evaporate.

The carrots should be perfectly cooked and just tender when the water has totally evaporated. Taste and add salt and pepper as needed.

In a very hot pan, pour some olive oil. When smoking, pan-fry the split shrimp for 1 minute. Add some butter and gently shake the pan so the butter coats the shrimp.

Pour the shrimp jus into the pan and serve in the pan at the table.

GRATED CARROTS WITH ORANGE & GINGER

Difficulty level: easy
Calories: 65
Preparation time: 15 minutes

Serves 4

6 oz. carrots

4 tablespoons extra-virgin olive oil

1 tablespoon freshly grated ginger

1 teaspoon brown sugar

1 orange (zest & juice)

½ lime (juiced)

1 teaspoon sweet soy sauce

Salt & pepper

½ bunch cilantro (chopped)

Wash, peel, and grate the carrots.

In a bowl, whisk together the olive oil, ginger, sugar, orange, lime, and soy sauce, and add salt and pepper.

In a soup plate, put some grated carrots and toss with the dressing. Sprinkle over some chopped cilantro and serve.

CARROT

BIG CARROT AU JUS COOKED IN FIG LEAVES

Serves 4

Difficulty level: mediumx
Calories: 140
Preparation time: 30 minutes

¼ cup extra-virgin olive oil

8 large carrots (washed, not peeled)

Salt

¼ cup chicken jus (page 29)

8 grape leaves

4 fresh figs (sliced)

Preheat the oven to 325°F.

In a pan, heat the olive oil until it gets really hot. Add the carrots and sauté them while making sure they don't brown. (We are just trying to fix their original bright color.) Add a pinch of salt and chicken jus, and cover.

After 7 minutes, remove the lid. The liquid will have almost disappeared and the carrots should be cooked. Remove the pan and let them cool down.

Meanwhile, on a greased baking sheet, line the grape leaves with the sliced fresh figs. Put a carrot on each leaf and wrap them up.

Cook in the oven for 5 minutes. The grape leaves will have turned crispy and the fresh figs will have softened over the carrots. Open up the wrapped leaves on a plate and serve.

BIG CARROT AU JUS COOKED IN FISH SKIN *(Pictured)*

Serves 4

Difficulty level: hard
Calories: 185
Preparation time: 45 minutes

¼ cup extra-virgin olive oil, plus more for frying

8 large carrots (washed, not peeled)

Salt

2 cups fish jus (page 31)

8 sea bass or sea bream skins (ask your fishmonger, they are usually free)

2 tablespoons unsalted butter

Follow the first part of the previous recipe but use fish jus instead of chicken jus.

After 7 minutes, remove the lid. The liquid should have almost disappeared and the carrots should be cooked. Remove the carrots from the pan and let them cool down on a dish. Lay the fish skins on a clean surface. Sprinkle some salt on them and place a carrot in the middle of each skin. Roll each carrot neatly in the fish skin.

Heat some olive oil in a large nonstick pan. When the oil looks as if it may start smoking, add the carrots rolled in fish skin. Put on low heat and slowly roll the carrots in the pan. When the fish skins start turning a little crisp, add the butter and let it turn brown. Delicately stir, making sure to coat each carrot in brown butter and serve when they all look brown and shiny.

CARROT & HONEY TART

Difficulty level: medium
Calories: 380 (for 2 helpings)
Preparation time: 6 hours

Serves 4

Tart base

1¼ cups all-purpose flour

1 teaspoon salt

1 tablespoon superfine sugar

9 tablespoons unsalted butter (cut into big squares at room temperature, softened)

1 egg

1 tablespoon water

Carrot filling

6 large carrots (peeled & cut into ⅛-inch-thick angled slices)

4 tablespoons good-quality liquid honey

4 eggs

3 tablespoons superfine sugar

2 tablespoons rum

Pinch salt

2 oz. fresh ricotta cheese

1 teaspoon ground cumin

1¾ cups low-fat milk

¾ cup plain probiotic yogurt (such as Activia)

Making the tart base

In a bowl, mix the flour, salt, sugar, and the butter by hand until you get a crumbly texture. Break in the egg and add the spoon of water. Continue working the mix until it comes together as a fragile dough.

Remove the dough from the bowl and continue working it in your hands on a floured and clean surface. Do not overwork the dough, as it is always better when it is a little crumbly rather than dense and elastic.

Cover the dough with plastic wrap and keep it in the fridge for at least 4 hours before using it.

Making the carrot filling

Preheat the oven to 325°F.

In a large pot, boil the carrots for 4 minutes and refresh them quickly in cold water so they retain their bright orange color.

In a sauté pan, slowly heat the honey and add the carrots. Stir, making sure to coat all the carrots with honey. Let the honeyed carrots cool down.

In a bowl, break the eggs, and add the sugar and the rum. Whisk them together with a pinch of salt. When the mix develops a white creamy texture, add the ricotta and the cumin. Continue whisking. Add the milk and carefully add the carrots.

With a rolling pin, flatten the dough and press it over a buttered tart mold. Fill the tart with the carrot mix and cook in the oven for 25 minutes.

Serve the tart warm with a little yogurt.

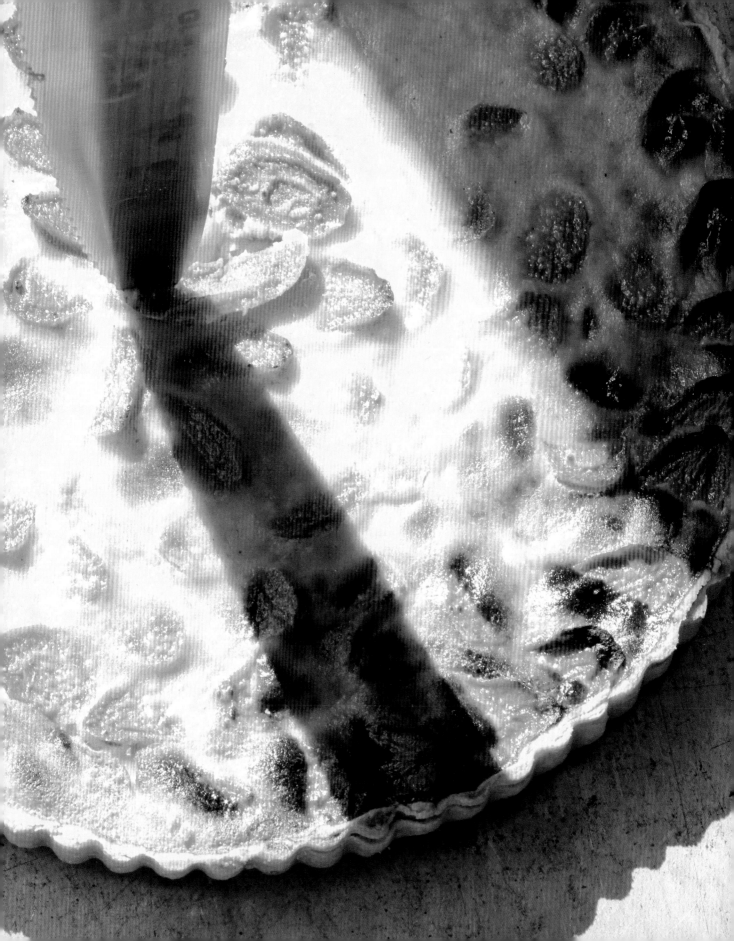

CAULIFLOWER GRATIN

Beef jus

Difficulty level: easy
Calories: 218
Preparation time: 45 minutes

Cauliflower is a weird vegetable: it has a difficult look. I have never heard anyone look at a cauliflower and say: "Oh, my God! I really need to have this now!" Children detest it and adults rarely crave it, except when they want to diversify their vegetable intake. It has an ugly shape and a bad smell, and it's uninspiring. It is the symbol of people refusing to eat vegetables. When I think about it, I think only about the cauliflower gratin my mother used to make. She always used condensed milk and it was the creamiest gratin I have ever tasted. It was also the lightest.

Also, she used to cover the gratin with the remaining jus of a roast, and that was just the most perfect thing that could happen to a tender cauliflower.

Buying the perfect cauliflower is pretty easy: its base must be very green and the flowers have to be spotless and very white.

Serves 4

- 2 cauliflower heads
- 2 tablespoons unsalted butter
- 2 tablespoons all-purpose flour
- 1¼ cups milk
- ½ cup unsweetened condensed milk
- 2 egg yolks
- Pinch mustard powder
- ¾ oz. grated Parmesan cheese
- 1½ oz. grated Cheddar cheese
- Pinch grated nutmeg
- Salt & pepper
- Remains of roast beef jus / ½ cup beef jus (page 30)

Wash the cauliflower, making sure to grate away any black spots.

Cut it up and cook in salted boiling water. It usually takes 4 minutes for cauliflower to be firm yet not fully cooked.

Remove the florets from the water and cool them under running water.

Heat a saucepan and melt the butter, then add the flour and let the mixture start to thicken. Add the milk and condensed milk (both cold). Cook for 3 minutes while constantly stirring and making sure that it is always gently boiling.

Remove the pan and wait until it cools down for 5 minutes.

Then add the egg yolks, mustard powder, grated Parmesan cheese, grated Cheddar, and nutmeg. Add salt and pepper to taste.

Line a gratin dish with the cauliflower and cover it with the mix.

Cook in a 350°F oven for 7 minutes and add the beef jus just before serving.

PIGGY CELERIAC

Difficulty level: hard
Calories: 280
Preparation time: 1 hour 30 minutes

Serves 4

- 2 small celeriac
- 18 slices maple-glazed bacon (or pancetta, or smoked bacon)
- ¼ cup extra-virgin olive oil
- 1 onion (peeled & diced)
- 1 shallot (peeled & diced)
- 1 very pale celery stalk (washed & diced)
- ½ cup red wine
- ¾ cup chicken broth
- 2 tablespoons unsalted butter
- 5½ oz. chanterelle mushrooms (washed, grated & pre-sautéed to remove excess water)
- Salt & pepper

Peel and wash the celeriac, making sure that you keep them whole. Boil in salted water for 15 minutes. Make sure that the celeriac are fully cooked but retain a little tenderness. Refresh and dry them out.

Cut 2 slices of bacon into small strips. With a small knife, insert the slices inside the celeriac. Be careful not to break the celeriac, but try to go as deep as possible.

Wrap the celeriac in the remaining slices of bacon. You can tie them up with string to make sure the bacon sticks to the celeriac during the remaining cooking process.

Preheat the oven to 325°F.

In a small sauté pan, heat the olive oil and add the diced onion, shallots, and celery.

Stir and add the wine. Let the wine evaporate for 1 minute, then place both celeriac on top of the garnish. Add the chicken broth. Remove the pan from the stove and put in the oven for 40 minutes.

Turn the celeriac every 10 minutes, so the cooking is even.

Just before taking the celeriac out of the oven, heat the butter in a sauté pan. When the butter turns brown, add the mushrooms and quickly pan-fry them for less than a minute. Add salt and pepper, and add them to the celeriac dish.

Serve the dish and carve the celeriac at the table.

CUCUMBER, GINGER & TARRAGON

Difficulty level: *easy*
Calories: 172
Preparation time: 30 minutes

Cucumber is famous for being the worst vegetable to digest, and on top of that it is one of the most tasteless. It is also the only vegetable my chefs can't stop playing with every time I get some delivered. Boys will always be boys! Personally, I love its shape, its very particular flavor, and its texture. I also like the fact that cucumber is rich in water and that it's very good if you are, like me, constantly trying to lose some extra pounds. I use cucumber both cooked and raw, mostly in the summer.

Serves 6

2 tablespoons sesame oil

Salt & pepper

2 cloves garlic (minced)

1 tablespoon superfine sugar

2 tablespoons tarragon / red wine vinegar

2 large cucumbers (peeled & cut into 2-inch-long strips)

2 oz. fresh ginger (peeled & minced)

½ bunch tarragon (roughly chopped)

½ tablespoon white sesame seeds

½ tablespoon black sesame seeds

When dressed with vinegar and sugar, cucumber shines by the power it has to combine two very strong flavors.

When it is served with a chilled and refreshing summer crustacean broth, cucumber tempers the power of shrimp, plus it also brings a vegetable aspect to the dish.

Into a large pot, pour the sesame oil, a pinch of salt, pepper, the garlic, sugar, and the vinegar. Then add the cucumber and bring to a boil. Remove immediately from the heat.

When the cucumbers are cold, transfer them to a bowl and cover with the fresh ginger. Toss until they are well coated, then add the fresh tarragon.

Sprinkle on some sesame seeds.

If used to accompany an apéritif, I usually plant a small wooden stick in each cucumber to facilitate the serving. Serve very cold.

CUCUMBER, ARUGULA, MINT & CHILLED SHRIMP BROTH

Difficulty level: hard
Calories: 160
Preparation time: 30 minutes

Serves 4

2 oz. black radishes

2 large cucumbers

16 small precooked shrimp

½ bunch fresh mint

¼ cup extra-virgin olive oil

Salt & pepper

3 oz. argula leaves

4 cups shrimp broth (chilled)

½ cup heavy cream (whisked until almost firm & kept in the fridge until serving)

Peel the black radishes and cut crosswise to get some very small and thin slices. Keep the slices in cold water in the fridge until serving.

Peel the cucumber neatly, making sure to remove the entire skin.

With a small, sharp knife, cut some small pieces of cucumber ⅛ inch thick. Keep them in very cold water until serving.

Peel the shrimp and put them in a large bowl. Chop some mint leaves and toss in with the shrimp and the olive oil, salt, and pepper. Then add the arugula and toss again, making sure that the leaves are well coated with oil.

Among 4 soup plates, divide the cucumber pieces and top them with the slices of black radish and arugula. Arrange the shrimp and place the remaining mint leaves over each plate.

Pour the broth on top and add a small dollop of cream.

GRILLED EGGPLANT

Shaved bonito, almond, sultanas, yogurt & shallots

Difficulty level: medium
Calories: 115
Preparation time: 45 minutes

Eggplant is often described as bland. Its real purpose is to act as a vehicle for other flavors while giving a very particular texture. I can't think of a similar texture that would come close to that of a cooked eggplant. I have found that two particular cooking techniques really enhance the beauty of an eggplant: grilling and baking.

Serves 4

2 large eggplants

1 head iceberg lettuce

½ cup extra-virgin olive oil

2 tablespoons balsamic vinegar

Salt & pepper

2 oz. plain probiotic yogurt (such as Activia)

1 shallot (peeled & thinly chopped)

1½ oz. sliced almonds (slightly colored under the grill)

1½ oz. golden raisins

2 tablespoons bonito flakes (see Note)

Wash the eggplants and cut them into ⅛-inch-thick slices. Grill each slice dry (without any oil) on both sides and rest on a clean dish towel. The eggplant should be soft but not dry or crisp.

Cut the iceberg lettuce into ¼-inch-thick slices. Line them on a tray and pour over the olive oil and vinegar. Make sure the lettuce is well covered. Add some salt and pepper and leave to soak for 10 minutes. The lettuce should absorb the oil and vinegar while retaining its crunchiness.

Meanwhile, pour the yogurt into a medium bowl and mix in the chopped shallot. Add some salt and pepper to taste.

Put the sliced lettuce on a plate and cover it with the cold grilled eggplant. Then cover with the yogurt and shallot mix. Sprinkle over the almonds and golden raisins and finish by adding the bonito flakes.

Note: Bonito is dried fish flakes, which tremendously enhance the original flavors they are associated with. Specialty markets often sell it, or you can order it from Amazon.

EGGPLANT BRUSCHETTA

Difficulty level: easy
Calories: 235
Preparation time: 1 hour

Serves 4

- 4 tablespoons extra-virgin olive oil, plus more for pan
- 2 large eggplants (cut into ¼-inch cubes)
- Salt & pepper
- 1 shallot (chopped very thinly)
- 1 clove garlic (chopped very thinly)
- 2 tablespoons red wine vinegar
- ½ cup chicken jus (page 29)
- 1 baguette

Preheat the oven to 350°F.

In a large sauté pan, pour some olive oil. When the oil starts smoking, add the eggplants with a pinch of salt and start to sauté them. Wait until the eggplant starts releasing its water but has not begun to brown. Drain the eggplant in a colander. Arrange it in a shallow roasting tray and cook in the oven for 8 minutes.

Cool down the eggplant and mix in a bowl with the shallots, garlic, 2 tablespoons of vinegar, and the olive oil. Mix well so the eggplant has the texture of a coarse mash. Taste for salt and pepper and add the chicken jus. Keep in the fridge until serving.

Set the oven to broil. Cut some slices of bread (¼ inch thick), brush some olive oil on both sides, and toast for 5 to 7 minutes, turning once to brown both sides.

When the bread is golden brown, serve it on a plate accompanied with the cold eggplant purée.

Endive can be white or red. The white is usually more bitter than the red. I like doing a cure of endive at the beginning of each year. I eat it raw before every meal. On top of making me chew like crazy, it also makes me visit the restroom more often than usual.

I clean the inside of my body for a good start to the year.

Endive connoisseurs are usually tempted by the ones from the end of the season, when the yellow chicory turns green and slightly curly. It is the perfect bitter vegetable.

ENDIVE

GRILLED ENDIVE

Consommé of peppered leaves & sautéed chanterelles

Difficulty level: medium
Calories: 110
Preparation time: 1 hour

Serves 4

2 red endive

2 white endive

¼ cup extra-virgin olive oil

3 tablespoons unsalted butter

½ leek (finely chopped)

2½ oz. clean chanterelle mushrooms

Salt & pepper

2 cups water

½ bunch sorrel

½ bunch flat-leaf parsley (chopped)

Start by choosing the hardest endive you can find, then slice them lengthwise and remove the tough part near the top of the slice. Dip them in olive oil and quickly grill them until they become almost black and slightly soft. Some of the leaves will turn crispy.

Into a large heated pan, add the butter. When it turns brown, throw in the leeks and chanterelles and stir vigorously. Add a pinch of salt. When the chanterelles start releasing their moisture, pour over the water and bring to the boil.

Prepare the sorrel by removing the leaves from the stem. Wash them and add the leaves to the chanterelle water. Cook for 1 minute at a slow simmer.

Serve this dish by putting the slices of endive slices in the middle of the plate. Scatter the flat-leaf parsley around the slices. Grind some pepper, and pour the stock together with the mushrooms and sorrel leaves over it.

ENDIVE

BRAISED CHESTNUTS & WHITE ENDIVE *(Pictured opposite)*

Difficulty level: medium
Calories: 170
Preparation time: 1 hour

Serves 4

- 6 white endive
- ½ stick (4 tablespoons) unsalted butter
- 150g vacuum-packed chestnuts
- Salt & pepper
- ½ cup extra-virgin olive oil
- ¾ cup chicken jus (page 29)

Wash the endive and dry them with a clean dish towel. Cut the endive into thick slices and keep them on a plate covered with plastic wrap (so they don't turn black). Heat some butter in a large pot and add the chestnuts when it turns brown. Stir and add salt. When the chestnuts are slightly caramelized, put the slices of endive on top, making sure that none touch the bottom of the pan. Add a bit of water and salt. Cover and cook slowly for 15 minutes. Check often whether the amount of water is sufficient to create steam for the endive to cook. Remove the slices of endive when they are cooked and put them in a gratin dish. Place the chestnuts on top (they should be smashed by then) and add the olive oil, the chicken jus, and some freshly ground black pepper. Serve hot.

WHITE ENDIVE SALAD WITH BLUE CHEESE, BACON, GRANNY SMITH & TOASTED ALMOND *(Pictured on pages 148–149)*

Difficulty level: easy
Calories: 235
Preparation time: 30 minutes

Serves 4

- 1 egg yolk
- 1 tablespoon Dijon mustard
- ½ cup grapeseed oil
- 2 tablespoons red wine vinegar
- 1 lemon (zest & juice)
- Salt & pepper
- 2 boiled eggs (peeled)
- 4 white endive
- 4 slices smoked bacon
- 1½ oz. sliced almonds
- 2 Granny Smith apples (cored & thinly sliced)
- 3 oz. blue cheese (crumbled into small pieces)
- ¼ cup extra-virgin olive oil

Start by making the dressing. Whisk an egg yolk with the mustard and emulsify it by slowly adding the grapeseed oil. Add the vinegar, lemon juice, salt, and pepper. Taste and add the boiled eggs. Mash them up with a fork so they give a real consistency to the dressing. Reserve for later use.

Detach the endive leaves from the bases and wash them thoroughly under very cold water. Dry them carefully with a clean dish towel. Then cut them in two lengthwise.

Heat a nonstick pan on high heat and pan-fry the bacon for 2 minutes on each side. Add the sliced almonds and sauté them with the bacon for 30 seconds. Remove from the pan. Toss the endive in a bowl with the dressing.

Divide the endive among 4 large plates and add the bacon, almonds, lemon zest, apple slices, and blue cheese. Add a drizzle of olive oil and serve.

FAVA BEAN

This is one of the most delicate of all the vegetables I use. The best time to eat fava beans is when they are very young, pale green, and very tender.

There is something dull about the fava bean, though. It takes an hour to peel two handfuls and just 3 minutes to eat them! Lucky are the ones who indulge on fava beans. They surely don't have to double peel them!

You can find fava beans from May to early September. Sadly, the late-season bean is not as sweet and tender as the early one.

You can prepare some superb cold fava bean soups when they become too astringent to be eaten raw.

These are three recipes for the fava bean: the first one is for the early season, when they are small, sweet, and pale green; two are for the end of the season, when they are too big, but still delicious when cooked.

FAVA BEAN

FAVA BEAN & CHERVIL SALAD ON TOAST *(Pictured)*

Difficulty level: easy
Calories: 277
Preparation time: 30 minutes

Serves 4

2¼ lb. fava beans (double peeled)

½ cucumber

8 small round radishes

2 oz. tinned tuna

2 tablespoons mayonnaise

1 lemon (juiced)

½ bunch chervil (chopped)

½ bunch flat-leaf parsley

Salt & pepper

¾ cup extra-virgin olive oil

¼ cup aged balsamic vinegar

4 slices rustic French bread (rubbed with garlic, oiled & toasted)

8 anchovy fillets

Remove the fava beans from their shells (or ask someone to do it for you!).

Boil some water in a big pan. Throw the fava beans into it, let them sit for 5 seconds, and drain. Refresh under cold water, put them on a clean dish towel, and remove their thin skin.

Peel and slice the cucumber with a Japanese mandoline. Wash and slice the radishes, also with the mandoline.

In a large bowl, gently mix the tinned tuna with the mayonnaise and the lemon juice, and taste. Add the chopped chervil and parsley and add a bit of olive oil. Taste for salt and pepper.

Put the fava beans in a bowl with the sliced radishes and cucumber. Combine the balsamic vinegar, salt, pepper, and about ½ cup olive oil, and drizzle over.

Cut each slice of bread into 3 long slices. Top each of them with the tuna mix, then add the fava bean mix.

Add some anchovy fillets, olive oil, salt, and pepper, and serve.

INFUSION OF FAVA BEANS WITH LEMON BALM

Difficulty level: easy
Calories: 120
Preparation time: 1 hour 30 minutes

Serves 4

12 cups water

½ carrot

½ onion

½ leek

2¼ lb. fava beans (unpeeled)

1 bunch lemon balm

Salt & pepper

¼ cup extra-virgin olive oil

This recipe should be used late in the fava-bean season, when the beans are very hard.

Into a big pot, pour the cold water with the carrot, onion, leek, unpeeled fava beans, and half the bunch of lemon balm. Add a bit of salt and cook for 1 hour.

Add the remainder of the lemon balm and allow to infuse. Remove the lemon balm and serve the broth hot with the stewed vegetables.

Add a splash of olive oil and some freshly ground pepper just before serving.

CHILLED SOUP OF LATE FAVA BEANS
Watercress & poached egg

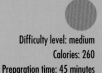

Difficulty level: medium
Calories: 260
Preparation time: 45 minutes

Serves 4

2 tablespoons olive oil

2¼ lb. fava beans (thickly chopped in their pods, about 1cm thick)

Salt & pepper

4 cups chicken broth (page 32)

White wine vinegar

4 eggs

½ bunch curly parsley

1 tablespoon sunflower oil

In a large pan, heat the olive oil. When the oil is smoking, throw in the chopped fava beans and stir vigorously in order to stabilize the chlorophyll in the beans without browning them.

When the fava beans are very green and shiny, add some salt and the chicken broth and put a lid on.

Cook for 7 minutes on a high heat. The fava beans should still be green after 5 minutes and should melt in your mouth.

Remove everything from the pan. Blitz in a food processor and pass through a large-holed colander. Discard solids.

Put it in the fridge overnight (minimum) and serve the following day. The flavor of fava beans tends to intensify when you leave the soup to rest for at least 12 hours before serving.

Boil some water in a deep pan. Add the vinegar. Break the eggs one by one into the boiling water and cook them for 3 minutes. Remove them from the water and refrigerate.

Quickly pan-fry the parsley in the sunflower oil.

Place a cold poached egg in the middle of each bowl and top with the crispy parsley. Pour the cold soup around and serve.

SOFT FENNEL SALAD

Lemon, parsley & yogurt sorbet

Difficulty level: medium
Calories: 150
Preparation time: 2 hours

Serves 6

Fennel

4 fennel bulbs

Sorbet

3 cups water

14 oz. granulated sugar

2 lemons (zest)

½ bunch parsley

3 cups lemon juice

1½ cups yogurt

Dressing

2 tablespoons mirin

2 tablespoons superfine sugar

2 tablespoons soy sauce

1 tablespoon balsamic vinegar

8 tablespoons olive oil

Preparing the fennel

Wash the fennel and cut away any black stains from the skins. Cut them in 2 and thinly slice them with a mandoline. Put them in icy cold water for 10 minutes, until they become crunchy. Dry them with a cloth.

Making the sorbet

Prepare the sorbet by bringing the water, sugar, and lemon zest to a boil.

Liquidize the parsley and add it to the lemon syrup and yogurt. Turn in an ice cream machine.

Making the dressing

In a bowl mix the mirin, superfine sugar, soy sauce, balsamic vinegar, and olive oil.

Serving the dish

Gently add the fennel slices to the dressing.

Divide between 4 plates and add some spoons of the sorbet.

FENNEL & EGG GRATIN

Lamb jus & thyme

Difficulty level: medium
Calories: 380
Preparation time: 1 hour

Serves 4

8 fennel bulbs (outer dark leaves removed & washed)

½ cup extra-virgin olive oil

Salt & pepper

2 cups chicken stock

2 egg yolks

¾ cup crème fraîche

1½ oz. grated Cheddar cheese

12 eggs (boiled for 10 minutes, peeled & sliced with an egg slicer)

¾ cup lamb jus (page 29)

3 sprigs thyme

Preheat the grill to 375°F.

Cut the fennel lengthwise in 2, then slice across about ½ inch thick.

In a large sauté pan, heat the olive oil until very hot. Add the slices of fennel, salt, and turn them around while letting them brown slightly. Add the chicken stock and cover. Cook for 6 minutes at high heat. Check if the fennel is cooked by inserting a knife into the bright white part of it. There should be no resistance.

Remove the fennel from the cooking pan. Transfer the cooking liquid into a bowl and add the egg yolks, crème fraîche, and grated Cheddar cheese. Taste and add salt and pepper if needed.

Line a buttered roasting dish with the slices of fennel. Cover with slices of boiled egg. Add the fennel juice mixed with the egg yolk and cheese. Pour the lamb jus over the dish and sprinkle with thyme.

Cook under the broiler for 4 to 5 minutes, until the dish looks golden brown.

Remove from the oven and serve immediately.

GARLIC

Garlic is one of the most ancient condiments we can find. It was used in China for its magical virtues. In Egypt, garlic was given to pyramid builders to prevent disease and provide them with extra strength. Good for the builders but bad for the Pharaohs, who banned garlic from their court because of its smell.

In Paris, people used to eat garlic on toast with butter because they thought that it was good for them. They didn't mind that garlic is hard to digest and not exactly great for social occasions because of your breath after eating it.

Garlic can be eaten raw or cooked. It can be cooked as a vegetable but is known primarily as a flavoring.

I was brought up in a garlic world. Garlic was everywhere around me. Meat cooked with garlic stuffed in every hole, fish wrapped in garlic leaves, garlic and bread soup during winter, garlic and milk when I was sick, and my mother's kisses before going to bed, which always smelled of a combination of garlic and blue Gauloise cigarettes.

CHILLED FAVA BEAN & GARLIC SOUP *Ricotta cheese*

Difficulty level: medium
Calories: 230
Preparation time: 30 minutes Resting: 4 hours

It is common knowledge in the South of France that you recognize good garlic and how wonderful it tastes when you belch it. A garlic tsunami submerging your entire nose and tastebuds is something you would look for. This recipe should not be served before important business meetings or romantic gatherings, but for garlic lovers it is heaven.

Serves 4

4½ lb. fresh fava beans

2 heads garlic

Extra-virgin olive oil

Salt & pepper

12 cups water

½ cup cream

2½ oz. fresh ricotta cheese

Chop half the fava beans (in their pods) to ¼ inch thick. Wash under running water for 5 minutes to make sure that all dirt is removed.

Peel the garlic heads (retaining a couple of cloves for presentation) and smash the cloves flat on a board with your hand. Pour some olive oil into a pan. When the oil is hot, add the garlic, making sure that it doesn't brown.

Add the chopped fava beans and stir vigorously. Make sure not to let the fava beans brown. When the beans are very shiny, add some salt, the water, and cream. Cover with a lid and cook for 12 minutes. Remove from heat and let cool slightly.

Blitz in a mixer for 10 minutes and pass through a large-holed sieve. The soup should have a creamy texture. If it is too thick, add a bit of cream mixed with salted water. Keep in the fridge for at least 4 hours before serving.

Peel the reserved garlic cloves, slice them, and slowly deep-fry them in oil so they become slightly crunchy and a little bitter. Double peel the remaining fava beans, making sure to remove every layer of skin. Once this is done, put them into a bowl and season with salt, pepper, and olive oil.

Place the fava beans at the bottom of the soup plate and add a spoonful of fresh ricotta cheese in each plate. Season the ricotta with some salt, pepper, and olive oil. Sprinkle the fried slices of garlic onto the dish.

Pour the very cold soup around and serve.

GARLIC & BAMBOO-STEAMED COD

Difficulty level: hard
Calories: 185
Preparation time: 1 hour 15 minutes

Golden croutons, Romaine lettuce & lemon dressing

Serves 4

For the cod preparation

14 oz. fresh cod fillet

¾ cup virgin olive oil (mainly for marinating)

Salt & pepper

20 cloves garlic (peeled and smashed)

2 slices of crunchy bread

2 heads of Romaine lettuce

For the dressing

2 tablespoons aged balsamic vinegar

2 cloves garlic

4 tablespoons extra-virgin olive oil

Salt & pepper

1 lemon (juiced)

You will need a Chinese-style steamer for this recipe.

Cut the cod fillet into 4 slices. Place the slices in a bowl and cover them with olive oil, salt, pepper, and the garlic cloves. Gently stir with a large spoon; make sure not to break the flesh.

Cover the bowl with plastic wrap and refrigerate for a minimum of 30 minutes. This way, the cod flesh will have enough time to absorb the olive oil and to let the garlic infuse it.

Meanwhile, cut the bread into small cubes and gently pan-fry until golden brown.

Cut at the base of the lettuce to release the leaves, and wash under very cold running water.

Remove the fillets of cod from the fridge and delicately place them into the bamboo. Make sure to first place the garlic cloves and "sit" the fish on top of them.

In a sauté pan, boil nearly 1 inch deep of water. Place the bamboo steamer in the pan and steam the fish for about 5 minutes.

Prepare the dressing by mixing the vinegar with the chopped garlic, olive oil, salt, pepper, and the juice of 1 lemon together in a large bowl. Toss the lettuce in the dressing and add the fried croutons.

Place the lettuce and croutons in the middle of each plate and top with a steamed slice of cod. Add the remaining lettuce on top and drizzle the remaining dressing over each fish.

Serve immediately.

GARLIC

AIGO BOULIDO *(Pictured)*

Serves 4

Difficulty level: medium
Calories: 160
Preparation time: 45 minutes

4 heads garlic (1 head per person)

8 cups water

4 sage leaves

1 bay leaf

1 tablespoon sea salt

Extra-virgin olive oil

Pepper

4 slices of rustic French bread
(preferably a little old)

½ bunch flat-leaf parsley
(roughly chopped)

This translates as *boiled garlic* from Provençe.

Peel the garlic and remove the cores within the clove. Cook them in the water with the sage, bay leaf, and salt until the garlic is soft (around 15 minutes).

Then remove the garlic from the stock and mash it in a bowl with a fork. Add a little olive oil until it gets the consistency of a paste. Add a pinch of salt and some pepper.

Let the stock reduce for an extra 15 minutes. Pass it through a sieve and season to taste.

Cut the bread into 1½ inch x 1½ inch squares and add a spoon of olive oil on each piece of bread. Toast the bread in a toaster or under the broiler.

Top the bread with the garlic paste and place each piece in a soup bowl. Add some roughly chopped flat-leaf parsley and pepper, and pour the garlic broth over.

Eat when very hot with a large splash of olive oil.

GARLIC JAM

Serves 4

Difficulty level: easy
Calories: 50
Preparation time: 1 hour

8 cloves garlic (peeled)

¾ cup condensed milk

2 teaspoons granulated sugar

Salt & pepper

Remove the cores in the garlic cloves and put the cloves in a pot filled with the condensed milk, sugar, salt, and pepper. Cook slowly until you get a thick paste.

Put this paste in the fridge and serve it on toasted bread as an appetizer (or for breakfast).

GARLIC PESTO DIP

Difficulty level: easy
Calories: 210
Preparation time: 30 minutes

There are two things you must accept the day you decide to start being taken seriously as a cook (home or restaurant). The first one is that your fingernails will never look the same as before (never trust a chef with perfect nails—he surely hasn't cooked for years). The second is that your hands will always smell of garlic. It is one of those smells that you can never really get rid of. When mixed with human skin, it penetrates and lingers even after days of intense washing.

Serves 4

1 large bunch garlic scapes

1 head garlic, peeled

½ bunch flat-leaf parsley

2 oz. toasted cashews

2 tablespoons finely grated Parmesan cheese

1 small red chile

½ cup olive oil

Salt & pepper

1 tablespoon white wine vinegar

Bunch small carrots or other dipping vegetables (peeled)

Place the garlic scapes, peeled garlic, parsley, cashews, and Parmesan cheese in a mortar and pound until well combined.

Finely seed and chop the red chile and add to the mixture.

Gradually add the oil in a thin and steady stream. Make sure that it turns into a thick paste. Taste and add salt, pepper, and the vinegar.

Transfer to an airtight container and pour over a little extra oil to cover the pesto surface.

Serve the pesto with some little raw vegetable sticks such as carrot, celery, white chard, or crunchy lettuce leaves.

LEEK

Winter or spring, the leek is one of the most important vegetables we can find in a kitchen. It is a basic ingredient in many preparations: stock, juice, soup, and much more.

It is also one of the oldest vegetables. The Egyptians loved it so much that they considered it a flower and used to give it as a present to good soldiers. In the Roman Empire, the leek was reputed to clear your voicebox. Nero used to eat a lot of it before his long and famous speeches. The Romans introduced the leek to Great Britain, and then the leek became the emblem of Wales.

Leeks are very rich in potassium and vitamins K and A, and they are an excellent diuretic. In my kitchen the leek is almost everywhere, especially in winter when it becomes hard to find a bit of green in vegetables. What gives me the most pleasure is to make it shine on its own. The leek doesn't need much help from any other ingredient or even any dressing.

The complexity of its texture makes it most interesting to work with. The leek is a complicated vegetable with thin layers of juicy tenderness in a shade of green. Steamed, boiled, pan-fried, or even deep-fried are just a few ways you can get the best from this kitchen pearl.

If this isn't enough to convince you that the leek is far superior as an ingredient to filet of beef, for example, you should remember that it is the perfect tool if you need to lose weight. Stuff yourself with leeks every day for a long period and you will see how your body changes.

My grandmother made it an annual ritual to feed herself solely with leeks for the first months of each year. She would then lose the extra pounds. She would serve them warm in a not-too-sweet and sour dressing.

This is most definitely the easiest way to fall in love with leeks.

SOFT LEEK

Yogurt vinaigrette, boiled egg, capers & anchovies

Difficulty level: medium
Calories: 90
Preparation time: 15 minutes

In this dish it is not the leek that brings its light and fresh fibrous texture for the anchovy to shine. It is completely the opposite. The whole dish is built around the soft texture of the leek and the other ingredients mainly make the leek look and taste even better without compromising its own specific refinement. Take a mouthful of all the ingredients and you'll see how they all play around the leek.

Serves 4

4 large leeks

½ cup olive oil

4 eggs

1 tablespoon Dijon mustard

1 tablespoon red wine vinegar

½ cup plain probiotic yogurt (such as Activia)

Salt & pepper

12 small anchovy fillets

2 tablespoons capers

Remove the darkest green part of the leek. If you buy your leeks from a supermarket, it may already be removed. Cut the leeks in half lengthwise and wash them. Do not be afraid to open them up in order to wash everywhere.

As with most green vegetables, you will be cooking the leeks by heating a bit of olive oil in a pan. When the oil is smoking, put the leeks in and shake the pan without flaming it until you have stabilized their chlorophyll without browning. Add a pinch of salt and water to cover. Top with the lid. Check often.

When the leeks are tender, remove the lid and let the juices evaporate. Then remove them and place in a large dish with the rest of the olive oil.

Cook the eggs in boiling water for 8 minutes. Peel them under running water (to make it easier).

Into a large bowl, whisk together the mustard and vinegar while pouring in the yogurt. Season with salt and pepper, tasting constantly until you think that the balance of acidity to sweetness is perfect for your taste.

Place the leeks faceup on each plate. Add the anchovy fillets and sprinkle over some capers.

Mash the boiled eggs while still warm. Then pour the vinaigrette over the leeks and top with the boiled eggs.

LEEK

GREEN LEEK JAM *(Pictured)*

Difficulty level: easy
Calories: 105
Preparation time: 45 minutes

Serves 4

6 oz. leeks

3 tablespoons unsalted butter

1 lime (chopped)

Indonesian long peppercorns

2 tablespoons sugar

¾ cup water

Wash and dry the leeks (especially the green ends).

In a large saucepan, heat the butter. When it turns brown, add the leeks, the lime, the peppercorns, and the sugar. Cover with water and slowly cook for 20 minutes.

Serve cold. It is superb with grilled fish!

LEEK, TRUFFLE & BONITO

Difficulty level: hard
Calories: 55
Preparation time: 30 minutes

Serves 4

20 small leeks

2 teaspoons Dijon mustard

2 tablespoons red wine vinegar

8 tablespoons sunflower oil

2 teaspoons black truffle oil

Salt & pepper to taste

1½ oz. black Perigord truffle

2 teaspoons bonito flakes
(see page 138)

Delicately clean the leeks by removing the dark and hard end parts. Also, remove their first skin, which is usually a little sticky.

In a bowl, combine the mustard and vinegar and start whisking slowly while adding the sunflower oil. Finish by adding the truffle oil, salt, and pepper.

Boil the leeks in salted water for 4 minutes. Drain and dry them as much as you can with a clean dish towel.

Place 5 leeks on each plate, add a few slices of black truffle on top, and pour the vinaigrette around. The leeks should be warm to be really enjoyed.

Sprinkle a few bonito flakes as you serve to accentuate the flavor of the truffle.

FONDANT LENTILS

Black & round radishes, leaves & mustard dressing

Difficulty level: medium
Calories: 230
Preparation time: 45 minutes

The lentil is a most nutritious ingredient. It is one of my favorite vegetables. I could eat lentils every day, all year long. Lentils are a great source of minerals and are rich in calcium, potassium, zinc, and folic acid. They are also perfect if you are looking to lose weight (well, as long as you only eat lentils). Lentils are considered a winter vegetable but I always argue against that point since I eat them all year round. I like them in winter as a lentil soup and in summer in a cold salad with chopped shallots and honey dressing.

Serves 4

- 3 oz. dried green lentils
- ½ onion, not chopped
- ½ leek (halved & washed)
- ½ carrot
- 1 bay leaf
- Pinch whole black pepper
- 1 tablespoon sea salt
- 1 teaspoon Dijon mustard
- 1 tablespoon red wine vinegar
- ½ cup olive oil
- 1 bunch round radishes (keep the leaves)
- ½ daikon or white radish

Place the lentils in a cooking pot and fill it with water. Bring to a boil, drain, and run under water until cold.

Put the lentils back in the pot and fill it with water, onion, the leek, the carrot, the bay leaf, and pepper. Cook at a very slow simmer.

Taste every 5 to 10 minutes until the lentils are almost melting between your teeth. You will, at this moment, realize that they are very undersalted. As with beans, if you salt during the cooking process, the lentils tend to break. It is just a matter of keeping the shape of the lentils intact. But on the other hand if you aren't bothered about that, then salt them as you put the garnishes on and add more, as needed, before serving.

In a bowl, whisk the mustard with the vinegar and olive oil. Add some salt and pepper and taste.

On a plate, pour a few spoonfuls of cooked lentils with a bit of their cooking stock. Place the radish leaves (washed) with some thin slices of daikon radish over the lentils. Then top with thinly sliced round radishes and pour over the dressing.

BREADCRUMBED TOFU & LENTILS
Sweet basil & chile dressing

Difficulty level: medium
Calories: 210
Preparation time: 45 minutes

I had a dream. A dream of making my children salivate when they saw tofu. A dream of seeing them ask for more. More tofu, please! Their natural reaction was total revulsion. They didn't like its look or its taste and its texture even less. However, after eating this dish of breadcrumbed tofu with basil, lentils, and shallots they have turned out to be completely hooked!

Serves 4

- 3 oz. cooked lentils (as in the previous recipe)
- 1 long shallot (peeled & thinly sliced)
- 1 bunch sweet Thai basil (chopped)
- ½ small chile (finely chopped)
- ½ cup olive oil
- 2 tablespoons balsamic vinegar
- Salt & pepper
- 1 egg
- 2 tablespoons whole milk
- 1 block firm tofu
- 2 oz. breadcrumbs

Cold, cooked lentils are perfect for this.

Put the lentils in a large bowl with shallots, most of the chopped Thai basil leaves, chile, olive oil, vinegar, salt, and pepper. Stir to get a tasty dressing mixed with the lentils.

Break an egg into a soup plate and mix in the milk. Dip the tofu in it and then transfer the tofu to another plate and cover it with breadcrumbs. In a frying pan, heat 1 tablespoon olive oil. When smoking, put the tofu in the pan and make sure that it cooks quickly without sticking to the bottom of the pan. After 2 minutes, remove it and put it on a cutting board. Slice it thickly and put the dressed lentils in between.

Put the tofu slices in the fridge for a couple of hours and serve cold with a large splash of olive oil on top, any remaining chopped basil, and a few drops of balsamic vinegar.

A SLIMMING PUNISHMENT

Simple and delicious punishments for having put on so much weight. A remedy for fatness.

SLIMMING LENTIL COCKTAIL

Difficulty level: easy
Calories: 80
Preparation time: 10 minutes

Serves 1

- 2 oz. cooked lentils (cold)
- ¼ cup soy milk
- 1 tablespoon white wine vinegar
- ½ cup water

In the bowl of a large blender blitz all the ingredients for 3 minutes, until you get a smooth consistency.

Don't expect this drink to look like your favorite triple-fat frappuccino. It's all about filling you up with lentils!

THE JUS OF A RED POTATO

Difficulty level: easy
Calories: 150
Preparation time: 20 minutes

Serves 1

- 6 oz. red potatoes
- 1 tablespoon honey

Peel the potatoes. Rub them against a cheese grater. Keep the juice and throw the rest away. You can add a spoonful of honey if you feel a bit disgusted by the cat's-tongue sensation in your mouth.

CARROT & ALOE VERA COLON CLEANSER

Difficulty level: easy
Calories: 35
Preparation time: 10 minutes

Serves 1

- 1 lemon (juiced)
- 1 large carrot (peeled & grated)
- ½ cup pure aloe vera water
- Pinch salt

You won't be on the road to rejuvenation unless you drink this delicious day-starter. No need for me to go into details of the wonderful consequence this drink will have on your digestion. The title says it all!

Warm the juice of one lemon. Add it to the bowl of a blender with the grated carrot, aloe vera water, and pinch of salt.

Blitz and drink straight after. Don't leave your house for the next 20 minutes.

WILD MUS

HROOM

Buying wild mushrooms from the market is the safest thing to do. It's best to actually get used to them in the market and then try to recognize them when walking in the woods.

Wild mushrooms are seasonal produce that are easy to use and to cook. They also bring a real depth of flavor to dishes. Their nuttiness and mineral taste can be enhanced by meat or fish jus.

They are real stars in my kitchen and are treated like royalty.

I would classify wild mushrooms in this order:

Porcini: many sorts of porcini mushrooms exist. The best ones are brown or bronze. The "tete-de-negre" is not bad either. They are available in late summer and autumn. They have their own section from page 200.

Chanterelle: this is my favorite wild mushroom. When cooked with brown butter it tastes divine.

Shiitake: this is in season during the months of April, May, and June only. It tastes fantastic when served with white dandelion leaves. It is almost bitter. In the mouth, it becomes almost sweet, thanks to the nutty and sweet butter it is usually tossed in.

Morel: too expensive and too good, they come in spring with the asparagus and are their best partner. Morel has to be eaten alone or with green vegetables such as green peas, fava beans, asparagus, sautéed romaine lettuce, or simply with a meat jus.

LIGHTLY CRUMBED MORELS

Veal jus, garlic & parsley

Difficulty level: medium
Calories: 330
Preparation time: 1 hour

This wild spring mushroom is probably the most exquisite mushroom a chef can cook with. Unlike truffles, which need to be served raw to be fully appreciated, morels need to be cooked to get the best of their texture and flavor. The gray-brown heads are conical, chambered, and have small wrinkles. Because morels contain less water than other varieties of wild mushrooms, they require liquid when cooked. You can therefore easily imagine that morels are perfect when combined with chicken or veal jus.

Serves 4

- ½ stick (4 tablespoons) unsalted butter
- 1 shallot (finely diced)
- 4 cloves garlic (smashed & finely chopped)
- 10 oz. fresh morels (washed 3 times to make sure no sand is left in their pores)
- Salt
- ¾ cup crème fraîche
- ½ cup chicken jus (page 29)
- ½ cup Panko breadcrumbs (they are very light; you can also use ordinary ones)
- 1 tablespoon clarified butter
- ½ bunch flat-leaf parsley (roughly chopped)

Their spongy texture soaks up the juice it is cooked in, so when you add a touch of cream it is unbelievable how the delicate texture of morels retains the juice in its wrinkled ridges.

It is complicated to find the exact cooking time a morel needs to hold on to the juice it has been cooked in while not becoming dry.

I have spent many years studying the cooking process of morels, but it was to my rational brain a little too rigid.

I have found over the years that morels are best cooked covered in an oven at 325°F for at least 30 minutes.

Preheat the oven to 325°F.

In a hot sauté pan melt a tablespoon of butter with the shallots and the garlic. Stir while making sure not to brown. Add the morels and continue stirring for 2 to 3 minutes. The morels will start releasing the little water they have. Add salt, crème fraîche, and chicken jus. Bring to a boil, then remove from the heat and pour into a gratin dish.

In a bowl mix the breadcrumbs with the butter and toss until the breadcrumbs are well coated and look shiny. Add the chopped parsley and cover the morels with this mixture. Cover the dish with a sheet of baking parchment and cook for 30 minutes.

Serve as soon as it is ready.

UMAMI BOMB

Difficulty level: hard
Calories: 310
Preparation time: 45 minutes

Parmesan & wild mushroom custard

I have heard everything about the fifth taste, the umami taste. My Japanese friends think they invented it. They seriously believe that they have been the only ones to use it for centuries. So now I read about the new intellectual gastronomes who rave about the deliciousness of umami and revere Japan for bringing this extra dimension to our enjoyment. Well, I can tell you that Brillat-Savarin had already managed in the nineteenth century to identify the deliciousness of food when he said, "Anything brown will always taste delicious in gastronomy."

Serves 4

- 2 tablespoons olive oil
- 3 oz. yellow chanterelle mushrooms (washed & roughly chopped)
- 3 oz. porcini mushrooms (washed & roughly chopped)
- 3 tablespoons unsalted butter
- ½ shallot (minced)
- 2 garlic cloves (minced)
- 2 thin slices pancetta (thinly sliced)
- Salt & pepper
- 1 whole egg
- ⅓ cup heavy cream
- 2 egg yolks
- ⅓ cup grated Parmesan cheese
- ½ cup whole milk
- ½ cup chicken jus (page 29)

Without going into too much depth about the process of transforming something good into something delicious, Brillat-Savarin had simply allocated a color to something the Japanese would later claim their own under the funny name of *umami*. This rich mushroom custard recipe is just what you need to know about umami with a traditional Western ingredients; the umami taste is explosive!

Preheat the oven to 300°F. Pour the olive oil into a hot pan and pan-fry the mushrooms for 1 minute, until they release their water. Drain and discard the cooking liquid.

Melt the butter in a thick-bottomed sauté pan. When the butter starts turning brown, add the shallots, garlic, and sliced pancetta. Stir and add the mushrooms. Add salt and pepper and stir for 2 minutes, making sure once again not to brown (otherwise the mushrooms will taste slightly bitter).

Remove the pan from the heat and transfer the mushrooms to a plate to cool.

In a bowl, whisk together the whole egg with cream, then add the egg yolks, Parmesan cheese, and milk. Mix well while making sure that all the eggs have been combined with the other ingredients. Add the mushrooms and stir well. Taste and add salt and pepper as needed.

Butter 4 ramekins or 4 short tumbler glasses and divide the mixture evenly among them. Place in a baking dish and pour cold water into the dish to reach halfway to the height of the ramekins or tumblers.

Cook in the oven for 25 minutes. Remove and allow to cool slightly while making sure that the custards are cooked by inserting a knife into one of them. If it comes out clean, it means that the custard is cooked. Just before serving, add a spoonful of warm chicken jus on top.

FLEXITARIAN. AM I ONE?

In a constant need to define who we are and express how we differ from one another as human beings, we have managed to fragment our race by how we feed ourselves.

The affirmation that we are what we eat will never be right in my eyes. Foods are not much more than just a collection of nutrients, especially in our current era; they do not possess a wealth of influences and connotations anymore, and we should be seriously happy about that.

It is very difficult for me to understand that some foods are worshipped in various cultures as having a special holiness, or are avoided altogether.

So with this state of mind, I found it very difficult to express what my preference really was.

Loving vegetables, while not stopping eating meat or fish, did not, until recently, have a name.

It was, to my eyes, absolutely normal to decide to indulge in plants rather than animals, just for the sake of pleasure.

Having spent many years looking at meat or fish as the centerpiece of a restaurant dish, I had been almost convinced to go against my natural inclination, which was having the vegetable as the leading product in a dish, and looking at meat or fish as just flavor tools.

So when I started creating menus in my restaurant with plants as the key to a dish, people loved it right away.

They were going crazy with what I was doing. They loved everything and they wondered how I could create so many different and delicious combinations of flavors.

"I was reincarnated as a half-baked vegetarian."

> ## "Loving vegetables, while not stopping eating meat, did not always have a name, until now."

Well, I believe that they loved it because I was cooking most of my vegetables in meat or fish stock. I would always add some grated tuna flakes or cured meat to broth, I would wrap carrots in duck skin to give them depth of flavor, I would cook stuffed tomatoes in the pan I'd used to make our beef jus, and so on.

I had never promoted my style of cooking as vegetarian, and yet was labeled as one of them. It took me many years to get myself the reputation of being a "Flexitarian."

But hold on a minute! That word is so new that even my computer doesn't recognize it.

So there I was, having managed to get rid of the Green Giant image, being reincarnated as a half-baked vegetarian.

Flexitarians are the unfinished children of vegetarians—the ones who were not quite brave enough to quit the world of animal eaters but for their good conscience have decided to carry the semi-dried Green Cross. They are the ones who can easily indulge with a Big Mac without having to repent for it.

They describe themselves as the third party of the eating world and never feel any guilt in eating smoked salmon but they will lecture you on the benefit their diet has on the rest of the world.

No, I am not part of the new age of eating. I may be as much a flexitarian as I am a vegetarian or a pure carnivore. But why is there any need for self-classification?

SWEET & SOUR RED PICKLED ONIONS

Difficulty level: medium
Calories: 140
Preparation time: 1 hour Resting: 5 days

Onions have been cultivated for the past 5,000 years. Their origins are in Persia, and the Egyptians were real fans. During the Roman Empire, the epicure Apicius used his favorite onions in many recipes. The onion is a condiment present all year long in my kitchen. It seems to me that it is one of those every-season kinds of vegetable. During winter it brings sweetness to our stocks and soups. In spring and summer I like to add it raw to dishes. It is beautifully crunchy and sharp in taste.

Serves 4

14 oz. small red onions

1¼ cups white wine vinegar

1¼ cups red wine vinegar

¼ cup granulated sugar

½ tablespoon salt

¼ teaspoon cayenne pepper

4 cloves garlic (sliced)

¾ oz. ginger (peeled & sliced)

3 sprigs fresh thyme

½ oz. fresh mint leaves

1 cup water

In the South of France, we cook the fish *au plat* (in a flat dish) and then add thin slices of onion on top of the hot fish. When you eat it, you feel that the onion has been slightly cooked but it retains its original crunchiness and the taste is enhanced.

Start by sterilizing 4 small (1 pint) jars and lids: wash them thoroughly and boil them in water.

Meanwhile, in a large cooking pot, put all the ingredients together and bring to the boil. Let them cook for 10 minutes.

Fill the jars with the onions and cover with the pickling liquid and garnishes. Make sure to leave about ⅛ inch of space in each jar. Place the seals and lids on each jar.

Boil them upside down in the water for 20 minutes.

Let them cool. The pickled onions will be ready to eat in 5 days.

ONION

ONION JAM

Difficulty level: easy
Calories: 90
Preparation time: 3 hours

Serves 4

- ¼ cup olive oil
- 6 oz. onions (thinly sliced)
- Salt & pepper
- ¼ cup brown sugar
- ¼ cup pomegranate syrup

In a small pan, heat the olive oil. Add the onion. Add salt, brown sugar, and pomegranate syrup and cover.

Cook very slowly for about 2 hours. Make sure to stir the preparation every 5 to 10 minutes. When the onions have the consistency of a compote, remove the pan and let it cool.

Add a bit of pepper and taste. You may want to add a bit more pomegranate syrup if you feel it lacks sweetness.

Serve cold.

ONION INFUSION

Difficulty level: easy
Calories: 0
Preparation time: 5 minutes

Serves 4

- 1 spring onion
- Boiling water
- Garlic cloves

You have to be like me to enjoy this: passionate about the taste of onions. I have to say that I have developed this recipe after getting some sort of craving for onions.

I usually take the greenest onion available (those which make you cry as you peel!) and cut them into thick slices when they are peeled. Boil some water and pour it over the freshly cut onion.

Inhale the smell by covering your head over the bowl with a dish towel. Beautiful!

Note: You can accentuate the smell by adding a few slivers of raw garlic to the onion. And somehow I am sure that it is also good for my health!

PEAS

Before coming to the UK in 1995, I could not understand the British love for peas. It was beyond my small, closed French understanding. I thought that peas eaten either mushy or overboiled in gravy were an absolute disgrace.

How on earth could you inflict such a barbaric treatment to the refined, small, sweet, and delicate little peas that I used to venerate when I was young?

I had never realized that peas had so many stages. I had been fortunate to be mostly fed with fresh, small, and sweet peas by my mother. I did not know that you could actually enjoy a riper pea.

I did not know that a mature pea could bring something substantial to a dish. I now enjoy peas in many more interesting forms.

Raw, early in the season with some lemon and wasabi dressing, quickly pan-fried with baby onions in the middle of its season, and mushy pea ravioli or in soup toward the end of the season.

I also now love the hard, tough, very late peas that you can almost braise so they become little sponges for the juices they are cooked in.

EARLY-SEASON RAW PEAS

Octopus & peas in a wasabi & lemon dressing

Difficulty level: easy
Calories: 240
Preparation time: 30 minutes

Serves 4

1 teaspoon wasabi paste sauce

1 lemon (juiced)

⅔ cup olive oil

6 oz. cooked octopus in oil sauce

1 lb. 2 oz. fresh peas in pods (or 6 oz. peeled)

Salt & pepper

3 oz. baby spinach leaves

In a small bowl, mix the wasabi paste with the lemon juice. Whisk in the olive oil until you get a light vinaigrette.

Cut the octopus into little pieces ¼ inch long and add them to the bowl with the vinaigrette.

Remove the peas from their shells and rinse under cold water.

Add them to the octopus and toss them together. Taste and add salt and black pepper.

Divide among 4 plates on top of some baby spinach leaves.

You can add a splash of olive oil and lemon juice just before serving.

END-OF-SEASON MASHED PEA RAVIOLI

Difficulty level: medium
Calories: 220
Preparation time: 3 hours

Serves 4

For the stuffing

- 1 lb. 2 oz. green peas in pods (or 6 oz. peeled)
- ¼ cup olive oil
- Salt & pepper
- ¾ cup water
- 1 egg
- 2 oz. ricotta cheese
- ¾ oz. or 4 teaspoons grated Parmesan cheese
- ½ bunch chervil, chopped

Ravioli

- 8 cups all-purpose flour
- 10 eggs
- 3 tablespoons water
- 1 tablespoon white wine vinegar
- Pinch salt
- A little grated Parmesan cheese

Making the stuffing

Remove the peas from their shells. In a large pan, pour a bit of olive oil and pan-fry the peas without browning. It is important to keep the peas very green. When they are very shiny, add some salt and water and cover.

The peas should be cooked after 3 minutes: test by putting one in your mouth. It should explode under the pressure of your tongue.

Put the peas on a plate and let them cool down a bit. Put them in a bowl and mash them with a fork or potato masher. Add the egg and mix. Add the ricotta, Parmesan cheese, and chopped chervil and mix with a wooden spoon.

When the stuffing is light but compact, add salt and pepper. Make sure you add a lot of pepper as it always accentuates the flavor of peas.

Making the ravioli

In a large vegetable bowl, place the flour, eggs, and the water. Mix with your hand until you get a dough of the same consistency all over. Add vinegar and salt and continue stirring with your hand.

Leave in the fridge wrapped in plastic wrap for a minimum of 2 hours.

Finishing the dish

Roll out the dough on a floured table. Cut some little rounds (2 inches in diameter) and put a spoon of stuffing in the middle. Wet the sides and press closed to seal them together.

Cook in boiling water for 2 minutes and serve in bowls with a large splash of olive oil and some more grated Parmesan cheese.

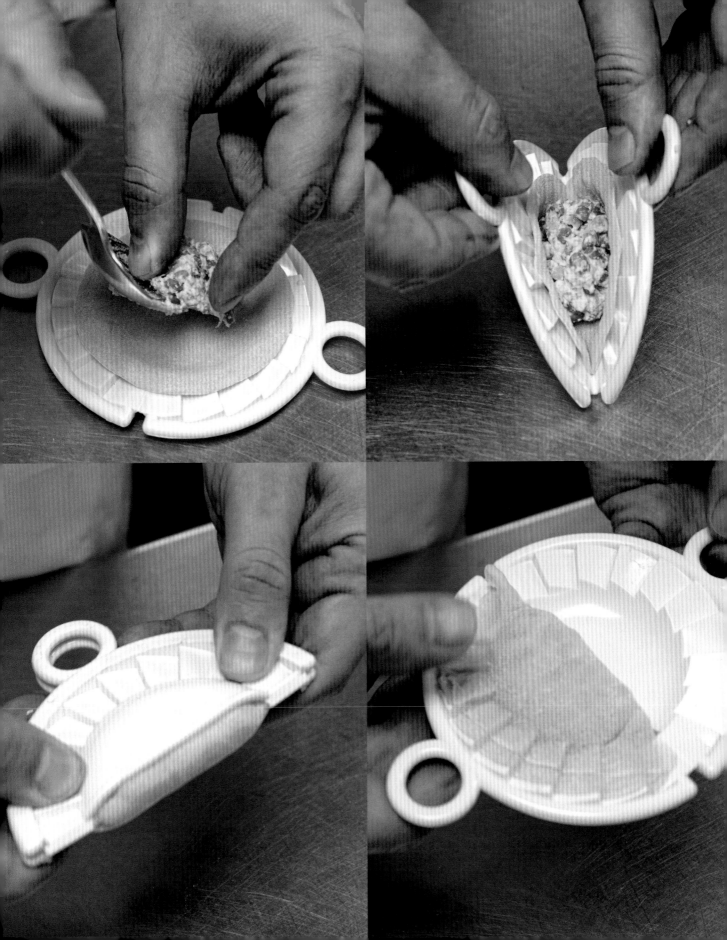

SAUTÉED GREEN PEAS

Pearl onion, sliced beef, purple basil & parsley

Difficulty level: easy
Calories: 180
Preparation time: 30 minutes

Serves 4

1 bunch purple basil

1 bunch flat-leaf parsley

¾ cup extra-virgin olive oil

5 oz. pearl onions (peeled)

14 oz. green peas (peeled & washed)

Salt & pepper

2½ oz. beef sirloin (thinly sliced à la carpaccio)

½ cup balsamic vinegar

4 teaspoons Parmesan cheese shavings

Remove the leaves from both the basil and parsley and keep them in a bowl with the water in the coldest part of your fridge.

Put a large pan on the stove and add a bit of olive oil. When the oil starts heating, add the onion and shake the pan until the onions are shining and then add some water. Cover and cook for 6 to 8 minutes, until the onions are meltingly soft when you put a knife through them. At this moment, add the peas to the onions and toss them together. Cover and cook for an extra minute at very high heat.

Check if the peas are ready. The green peas are cooked when a slight pressure under your tongue makes them explode in your mouth. At this stage, there should not be much liquid left in the pan. Add the fresh herbs to the pan, and add salt and pepper.

Prepare 4 large plates with slices of beef covering each of them. Spoon the onion and peas over the raw beef and top them with the herbs. Pour over the olive oil and balsamic vinegar and add some Parmesan shavings.

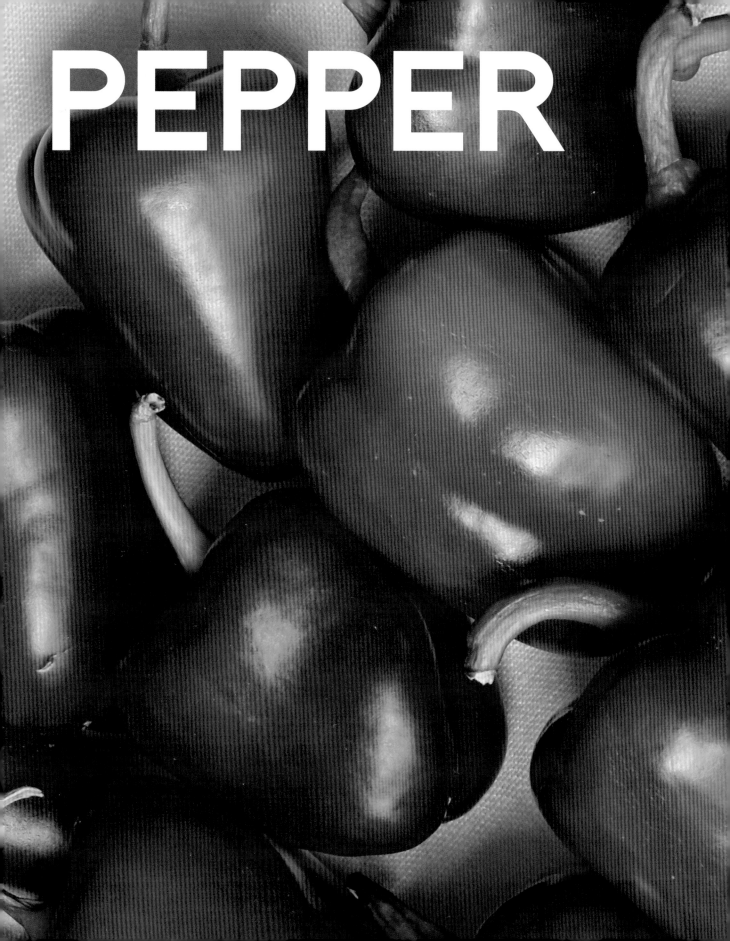

PEPPER

It's not difficult to find a perfect red pepper these days. They are sold when asparagus are at their best and also when chestnuts are in full swing. Red-pepper season is absolutely lost. I doubt that anyone remembers that summer is the best time to enjoy them.

Toward the end of June or in early July, red peppers give off a very particular green smell: a smell that tells you that peppers are sweet and juicy. It tells you that they have grown outside and have had some REAL sun. No lamps!

To choose a good pepper, you must look for the shiniest one with the tightest skin. As much as I love the smell of fresh and in-season pepper, there is one thing I can't do with them.

I can't eat them raw. They are just impossible to digest. Even the tiniest piece of red pepper will make me burp for hours and, unlike garlic or leek, the smell of the pepper burp is seriously embarrassing.

First of all, you must know that you should always remove the stem, skin, and seeds of the pepper before using it in any recipe.

There are two simple ways to remove the skin. The first is to plant a fork in the red pepper and place it over an open flame. Make sure that the skin turns dark and rotate the pepper until all four sides are cracked and burned.

The second technique is probably safer: place the pepper in a steamer for 8 to 12 minutes. Remove and throw into icy-cold water. The skin will slowly come off. You may need to use a knife to remove some of the smaller pieces of skin.

RED PEPPER

Anchovies, almond, thyme & rice

Difficulty level: medium
Calories: 237
Preparation time: 45 minutes

Serves 4

- ⅔ cup extra-virgin olive oil
- 1 small onion (peeled & chopped)
- 6 oz. long-grain rice
- Pinch salt
- ½ cup dry white wine
- 4 sprigs thyme
- 1¼ cups water
- 12 anchovy fillets (roughly chopped)
- 1½ oz. walnuts (broken into small pieces)
- 2 oz. sliced almonds (slightly roasted)
- 12 small red peppers (cut to retain the top, peeled & seeded—see previous page)
- 3 large potatoes (cut into 4 slices of ¼ inch each)

This is one of my favorite recipes.

Preheat the oven to 325°F.

Into a hot sauté pan, add some of the olive oil and the onion. Stir on a slow heat, making the onions become shiny without browning. Add the rice and a pinch of salt. Continue stirring on a low heat until the rice is shiny and very hot. Add the white wine and the thyme. Add the water and cover. Cook for 7 minutes on a very low heat.

Remove the rice from the heat and let it cool down for 5 minutes. In a bowl mix the anchovies, walnuts, almonds, and rice together with more olive oil. Fill each red pepper with the mix and put them each on a slice of raw potato in a roasting pan. Cook in the oven for 30 minutes.

Serve on a large plate accompanied by a salad of seasoned arugula salad.

PORCINI

Among all mushrooms, the porcini is probably the most chef friendly. It leaves plenty of room for creation. It can be served raw, cooked, as a soup, and I have even seen menus with porcinis as a dessert! Not sure that would work, but you never know.

You need to get hold of fresh porcinis just after they have ripened, when they're firm and not yet infested with worms. Their nutty flavor is incomparable and they are really the essence of the woods as far as I am concerned.

Over the years, the porcini mushroom has lost a bit of its aura mainly because of tinned porcini purée and oil infused with dried porcinis, which have been overused and have seriously compromised the integrity of this mushroom.

I hope these simple but delicious recipes will make you realize that the porcini is still one of the greatest wild mushrooms available.

CREAM OF PORCINI

Chervil & raw porcini mushrooms

Difficulty level: medium
Calories: 180
Preparation time: 30 minutes

Serves 4

2 tablespoons butter

10 small porcini mushrooms in good condition (washed, heads & bodies separated)

1½ oz. onion (chopped thinly)

4 cloves garlic (chopped thinly)

Salt & pepper

¾ cup crème fraîche

2 cups chicken broth (page 32)

1 bunch chervil (roughly chopped)

¼ cup olive oil

Melt some butter in a small pan with the porcini stems and half of the heads. Add the onion and garlic and slowly cook at low heat until the mushrooms start softening and releasing their water (this should take approximately 2 to 3 minutes). Add some salt and stir again. Pour in the crème fraîche and bring to a boil. Add the chicken broth and cover. Cook for 5 minutes at low heat.

Remove the pan from the heat and let cool slightly. Pour the contents into a blender. Blend until very thin without any chunks. The consistency should be one of thick cream. Taste and add more salt if needed. Do not add pepper just yet.

Divide the soup among 4 hot soup plates, sprinkle the chervil over each plate, and thinly slice the remaining heads of fresh mushrooms over each plate.

Add salt, pepper, and a splash of olive oil.

Serve immediately.

PORCINI & BACON

Chestnut leaves & veal jus

Difficulty level: hard
Calories: 150
Preparation time: 30 minutes

Serves 4

4 large chestnut leaves (washed & dried; collect these during the fall, or at your farmers' market)

8 slices smoked bacon

1 shallot (minced)

2 tablespoons unsalted butter

4 large fresh porcini mushrooms (lightly grated, washed & dried)

½ cup veal jus (available at your butcher's counter)

Preheat the oven to 325°F.

Lay the chestnut leaves flat on a clean surface. Cross 2 slices of smoked bacon on top of each leaf. Place some minced shallot, a little butter, and the mushrooms. Delicately close each mushroom in its leaf and place in a buttered roasting dish.

Cook for 15 minutes. Serve them opened up in the leaf with a little veal jus. The meat jus will absorb all the deep flavors together and will create osmosis between all the ingredients.

Is there any other dish that symbolizes the autumn in a more flexetarian way?

MASHED POTATO WITH CHERVIL & OLIVE OIL

Difficulty level: medium
Calories: 330
Preparation time: 45 minutes

Everything has been said about potatoes. We know that they are rich in potassium, vitamins B$_3$ and C, and folic acid. When I was under the weather, my mother used to grate a potato and make me drink the juice. The same beverage was prepared before an exam or a rugby match. I didn't really like it because its taste was very bland and the texture was strange. Like sucking a cat's tongue! I preferred the potato purée she used to make with olive oil and chervil. My mother's favorite potato was the Bintje potato from the Netherlands: perfectly yellow, moist, and easily breakable once cooked.

Serves 4

2 large potatoes

2 tablespoons sea salt

½ cup extra-virgin olive oil

½ bunch basil (roughly chopped)

Salt & pepper

2 bunches chervil (roughly chopped)

½ cup chicken jus (page 29; optional)

4 teaspoons grated Parmesan cheese (optional)

Wash the potatoes under cold water, making sure to remove any dirt. Put them in a large pot, fully covered with water. Add the sea salt and cook at a slow simmer for about 20 minutes.

Check from time to time with a small knife to see if the potatoes are cooked. The potato is cooked when there is no resistance to the knife.

Remove the potatoes from the water and peel them while very hot.

Put them back in the pot with a little water and salt.

Start smashing them with a fork while pouring in some olive oil. When the potatoes are puréed, add some more oil and carry on smashing with a fork. Add the chopped basil and some freshly ground pepper.

Taste and add more salt or pepper as needed.

Don't be afraid to put in a lot of chervil—it will taste even better.

Serve it as it is or add a splash of chicken jus and a sprinkling of grated Parmesan cheese if you like.

YUKON GOLD POTATOES

Cooked in brown butter with Parmesan cheese & flat-leaf parsley

Difficulty level: easy
Calories: 200
Preparation time: 30 minutes

Serves 4

2 tablespoons unsalted butter

24 small Yukon gold potatoes

Salt

1¾ cups chicken broth

2 oz. grated Parmesan cheese

1 oz. Panko breadcrumbs (because they are very light; you can also use ordinary ones)

½ bunch flat-leaf parsley

Preheat the oven to 425°F.

Put the butter into a thick-bottomed pan. Heat until the butter turns brown, then add the potatoes. Stir and add salt. The potatoes have to be uniformly brown. Add the chicken broth and put in the oven for 15 minutes.

Check that the potatoes are perfectly cooked all the way by slightly pressing on their skins.

Remove the pan from the oven and put the potatoes in a serving dish. Reduce the juice left in the pan until it gets thicker and pour over the potatoes with some grated Parmesan cheese, Panko breadcrumbs, and parsley.

You can serve this dish with a simple lettuce salad.

When autumn comes, so does the pumpkin! The sight of a pumpkin reminds me that summer is over and autumn is here. I like pumpkin. First, I like its shape. I like its enormity. When I was young, I remember going to the vegetable market with my mother. I was horrified by the sight of this giant "melon." On top of that, I hated the sight of its inside: full of scary orange hair. I didn't like to be near it. But since then, I have discovered its taste and texture, and the pumpkin has become a great friend.

The first time I had to cook a pumpkin was when I was in Monte Carlo. They do the most fantastic pumpkin risotto: very creamy, shiny, and rich. I realized that pumpkin was a top ingredient. Since then, I have always heavily featured pumpkin during the autumn months.

The pumpkin always stands next to the best ingredients available on the menu. It is often a starter on its own: polenta pumpkin with chicken jus or roasted with baby red chard and bergamot dressing.

In main courses it becomes the best partner for venison and truffle, or as a cream with steamed John Dory. It can also be a fantastic dessert, such as the pumpkin cake I used to prepare while in San Francisco for Halloween.

Pumpkin seeds are also great. When roasted they are better than any other roasted seeds. The Greeks and Romans used to make a body lotion out of them. They used it for its anti-aging properties as well as its nourishing qualities.

Pumpkin is the Autumn King.

PUMPKIN

PUMPKIN & CUMIN SOUP

Ricotta gnocchi & Parmesan cheese

Difficulty level: medium
Calories: 140
Preparation time: 1 hour

Serves 4

Pumpkin soup

1 lb. 2 oz. pumpkin

¾ cup extra-virgin olive oil

Salt

½ cup half-and-half

¾ cup chicken broth (page 32)

White pepper

Ricotta gnocchi

5 oz. fresh ricotta cheese

1 tablespoon cornstarch

1 egg

4 teaspoons grated Parmesan cheese

Salt & white pepper

To serve

Grated Parmesan cheese

1 teaspoon ground cumin

Making the pumpkin cream

Preheat the oven to 400°F.

Cut the pumpkin carefully into very big chunks with the skin on. Place the pumpkin chunks onto a tray and pour the olive oil over the chunks. Do not add any liquid, as the pumpkin will release its water under the heat of the oven. Put the pan in the oven for 15 minutes. The pumpkin should be soft and have a pale golden-brown skin over the flesh. Let the pumpkin cool down. Spoon the flesh out and put it in a blender. Blend until the purée looks free of any lumps.

Boil the cream and the chicken broth together with a pinch of salt and some white pepper. When it boils, add it to the pumpkin pulp. Taste, add salt and pepper as needed, and put to one side.

Making the ricotta gnocchi

In the bowl of the blender, put the ricotta, cornstarch, egg, Parmesan cheese, salt, and white pepper. Make sure all of the ingredients are well mixed together.

Transfer to a small bowl and keep in the fridge for 4 hours or in the freezer for 30 minutes.

In a medium saucepan, boil water with a pinch of salt and keep it at a simmer. Take a spoon of the gnocchi mix and plunge it directly into the boiling water. The heat and water will lift the mix from the spoon. Let the gnocchi boil for 2 minutes and delicately remove them before putting them onto an oiled plate.

Reheat the soup. Place the gnocchi into each plate sprinkled with a little Parmesan cheese. Pour the soup into the plate and add a pinch of cumin on the side.

PUMPKIN RISOTTO

Difficulty level: hard
Calories: 425
Preparation time: 1 hour

Serves 4

2½ oz. onion

¾ cup extra-virgin olive oil

9 oz. Italian risotto rice

Salt & pepper

½ cup white wine

4 cups hot chicken stock

14 oz. pumpkin

1½ oz. mascarpone

2 tablespoons unsalted butter

⅔ cup grated Parmesan cheese

¼ cup heavy cream

¼ cup beef jus (page 30)

Thinly chop the onion and heat it in a pan with 2 tablespoons olive oil until it becomes translucent.

Add the rice and a pinch of salt and warm the rice up to the point that you cannot touch it.

Stir without stopping and pour over the white wine. Start pouring in the chicken stock slowly for 5 minutes. The rice has to swim all the time in the same amount of liquid at a very slow simmer. After 5 minutes, drain the rice and spread it thinly on a tray in order to make it cool down quicker. Make sure to keep the cooking juice from the rice. It is indispensable when you finish cooking the risotto later.

Peel the pumpkin with a very sharp knife. Mind your fingers while peeling the pumpkin. You need to concentrate on your movement.

Make sure to remove all the "hair" and seeds left in the pumpkin. Thickly chop the pumpkin. Pour some olive oil in a pan and add the pumpkin. Stir without browning, add some salt, cover, and cook at a low heat. You do not need to add water because the pumpkin is very moist. After 6 to 7 minutes the pumpkin should be cooked. Retain 12 small pieces of pumpkin for serving. Remove the cover and stir the pumpkin in order to dry it out slightly.

Blend the pumpkin in a food processor and put the purée to one side.

Put the rice in a pan with the pumpkin purée and 2 cups of rice jus. Bring to a boil and then start to incorporate the ingredients one after the other, making sure they stay simmering.

First, add a spoon of mascarpone, then the butter, Parmesan cheese (2 tablespoons), the remaining olive oil, cream, salt, and pepper. Serve immediately.

The risotto has to be wavy—not hard and not soft, just in between. It is actually the olive oil added at the end that will make the difference. It will make your risotto stay creamy!

Divide the risotto among 4 soup plates, topped with the retained pieces of pumpkin, and pour beef jus around. Finish with a sprinkle of Parmesan cheese.

PUMPKIN & ORANGE BLOSSOM CAKE

Difficulty level: medium
Calories: 450
Preparation time: 2 hours

Serves 6

1½ lb. pumpkin (peeled and seeded)

7 tablespoons unsalted butter

¾ cup whole milk

⅓ cup granulated sugar

¼ cup plus 2 tablespoons cornstarch

1 teaspoon orange blossom water

Salt

3 eggs

9 oz. ground almonds

Heavy cream, for serving

Cut the pumpkin into small squares, cover, and cook them in a frying pan with 3 tablespoons of butter for 20 minutes.

Transfer to a blender and purée. Add the milk, sugar, and 4 tablespoons butter.

Mix well, transfer to a saucepan, and bring to a boil. Dissolve the cornstarch in water, add to the pan, and cook for another 2 minutes.

Remove from the heat and cool. Add the blossom water and a pinch of salt.

Separate the egg yolks and the whites. Add the three yolks to the pumpkin preparation one at a time. Whisk the whites until stiff and incorporate them slowly. Add the ground almonds delicately. Cook for 45 minutes in a buttered 8-inch cake pan at 350°F.

Serve warm with fresh cream.

GARDEN

SALAD

When picked young, lettuce has some beautiful fresh flavors and smells like fresh grass. It is also very refreshing and its light crunchiness is subtle in the mouth.

Lettuce is very easy to grow in the garden. It does not require special soil or a lot of space. There are many companies selling garden salad seeds.

Growing your own salad is something very special and you will feel a lot healthier. The best way to eat garden leaves is in salad. You can cook winter lettuce, but if possible always eat it raw.

SALAD DRESSINGS

Difficulty level: easy

Garden salad is and will forever be a part of my daily meal. Depending on my mood, season, or even the kind of dressing, I would use a different kind: curly, bitter, very pale, bright and full of chlorophyll, or just plain crunchy for the pleasure of chewing. I love the diversity: either wild or cultivated, lettuce has always been in my kitchen.

LEMON & MUSTARD DRESSING

Calories : 95
Preparation time: 10 minutes

Serves 4

2 frisée lettuce

2 tablespoons Dijon mustard

2 lemons (juiced)

¾ cup extra-virgin olive oil

¼ cup red wine vinegar

Salt & pepper

My mother made sure that we ate a decent amount of fresh salad on a daily basis. She used to prepare classic grain mustard vinaigrette to go with it. My uncle Henry liked lemon vinaigrette. Extremely acidic and always paired with plenty of black pepper. It took me many years to enjoy it. I am now absolutely addicted to this lemon dressing. His favorite salad to go with this acidic dressing was the frisée (or oak leaves) with tough stems and bitter yellow curly leaves.

Clean the frisée by removing all of its green leaves. Wash under cold water and drain until dry. Whisk the mustard and lemon juice together. When you start to get a thick paste, slowly add the olive oil, making sure that it doesn't separate.

Add the vinegar and the salt and pepper. Toss the salad in the bowl and serve.

BLACK TRUFFLE & CHICKEN JUS DRESSING

Calories: 319
Preparation time: 30 minutes

Serves 4

1 hard-boiled egg

1 teaspoon strong yellow mustard, such as Colman's

1 tablespoon fresh black truffle (chopped)

¾ cup extra-virgin olive oil

Salt & pepper

¾ cup truffle oil

¾ cup chicken jus (page 29)

2 bunches romaine lettuce

Romaine is the best—crunchy light-green leaves, and when coated in a truffle vinaigrette with chicken jus it is absolute heaven.

In a large salad bowl, break up the hard-boiled egg with a fork until you get it to a mushy texture. Add the mustard and the chopped black truffle. Pour in the olive oil. Add the salt, pepper, and truffle oil.

Reheat the chicken jus.

Divide the lettuce among 4 large plates. Pour the dressing over the salad and finish with a spoon of chicken jus on each plate.

GREEN SALAD

RED LEAF LETTUCE, GRAIN MUSTARD DRESSING

Serves 4

Difficulty level: easy
Calories: 70
Preparation time: 10 minutes

1 egg yolk

3 tablespoons grain mustard

¾ cup extra-virgin olive oil

3 tablespoons white wine vinegar

Salt & pepper

2 bunches red leaf lettuce

When you choose a green salad, make sure that the leaves are thin, smooth, and crunchy. The salad should be heavy and spotless. The sooner you eat it, the better it is when it comes to salad. The one I come across quite often is red leaf: it tastes really sweet and is always delicious when tossed with grain mustard dressing.

In a salad bowl, whisk the egg yolk slowly with the grain mustard. When it starts looking like a brownish paste, slowly pour in the olive oil. Whisk in the white wine vinegar, salt, and pepper. Toss with the lettuce and serve.

BRAISED LETTUCE, BEEF JUS & GOLDEN CROUTONS *(Pictured)*

Difficulty level: hard
Calories: 190
Preparation time: 30 minutes

Serves 4

3 butter lettuce

2 tablespoons unsalted butter

1½ oz. onion (chopped)

2 cloves garlic (chopped)

3 oz. carrot (chopped)

3 oz. pearl mushrooms (chopped)

Pinch salt

4 cups chicken broth (page 32)

¾ cup beef jus (page 30)

2 slices white bread (cut into small cubes)

¼ cup extra-virgin olive oil

Wash the lettuce by removing one layer of the outside leaves. Remove 2 unstained leaves on each lettuce head. Boil them for 5 seconds in order to stabilize their color. You will use them to wrap the braised lettuce at the end.

Boil the whole heads of lettuce in water for 1 minute and refresh them in cold water (the heads of lettuce will have seriously reduced in size).

In a large pan, slowly heat the butter and when it starts foaming, throw in the onion, garlic, carrot, and mushroom. Add salt and stir at a low heat. Lay the lettuce on top and cover with chicken broth. Cover with a lid and slowly cook for 15 minutes. Remove the lid and let the liquid evaporate.

Wrap each lettuce head (with a spoonful of vegetable garnish) in 2 quickly boiled lettuce leaves. Lay them on an oiled serving tray and drizzle some warm beef jus over.

Serve with golden brown cubes of white bread pan-fried in olive oil.

Salsify is a root vegetable commonly found at farmers' markets from November until February. It is almost impossible to find it in a supermarket. You may be able to find it in a tin but never fresh.

The reason is that people do not know how to use it. It is difficult to peel and takes a long time to prepare.

I also think that a big problem stems from the fact that most chefs and cookbooks tell you to boil salsify in water in order to cook it. So it never tastes really memorable.

I mean that you should never boil a root, but always simmer it in water and butter. It is the only way to cook it: it will be moist, tender, and full of flavor.

Another annoying thing is that those cookbooks tell you to rub salsify with lemon once peeled to stop it turning black. As with the artichoke, it is absolute nonsense to use lemon since you want to retain the original taste, and that has nothing to do with lemon.

Put them in icy water and cook them just after peeling.

SALSIFY

FONDANT SALSIFY

FONDANT SALSIFY & MARROW GRATIN

Serves 4

Difficulty level: medium
Calories: 320
Preparation time: 1 hour

14 oz. salsify

1¾ sticks (14 tablespoons) unsalted butter

5 cups water

Salt & pepper

8 veal marrows (boiled in salted water for 3 minutes & refreshed)

Grated Parmesan cheese

½ cup beef jus (page 30)

Wash and peel the salsify and put in icy water.

In a large, thick-bottomed pan, put the butter, salsify, and water. Add some salt, cover, and cook for 20 minutes. After 15 minutes, start checking the salsify by testing their resistance with a knife. If there is still resistance, it means that the salsify is not completely cooked. You need to be careful, as once the salsify is ready, it turns to mush very quickly.

Remove the salsify one by one and lay them on a baking sheet. Reduce the cooking juice until it gets quite thick, and pour over the salsify.

Preheat the oven to 350°F. Slice the marrow and place on top of the salsify. Add some pepper, sprinkle over some Parmesan cheese, and add the beef jus. Bake in the oven for 10 minutes and serve.

FONDANT SALSIFY & CRAYFISH *(Pictured)*

Serves 6

Difficulty level: hard
Calories: 310
Preparation time: 1 hour 30 minutes

10 oz. salsify

1¾ sticks (14 tablespoons) unsalted butter

5 cups water

Salt & pepper

½ cup shrimp jus (page 31)

¼ cup cream

20 crayfish (cooked for 5 minutes in salted boiling water & peeled)

½ bunch flat-leaf parsley (roughly chopped)

½ bunch cilantro (roughly chopped)

Cook the salsify as in the previous recipe.

Into a small pan, pour the shrimp jus and the cream. Boil them together and add the salsify and crayfish. Cover and slowly cook for 3 minutes.

Remove the cover and finish by tossing them together with a bit of pepper.

Plate the salsify and crayfish together and sprinkle with parsley and cilantro.

Pour the remaining jus around and serve.

TOMATO

The smell of a raw tomato is something you will never forget. Every time I come across tomatoes I have to smell them. Most important, I smell their stalks. It reminds me of Avignon, where I grew up, and where tomato is used in almost every dish.

When I was young, from March until October I would eat tomatoes in all their various forms for lunch and dinner—they would be served in soup, salad, stuffed, as a starter, a main course, and even as a dessert.

Tomatoes are good for me, and I need them.

Apparently, eating large quantities can interfere with calcium absorption, but I have never felt anything wrong despite consuming them in very large quantities.

A tomato is rich in magnesium, phosphorus, folic acid, and vitamin C. It is also a good antiseptic and reduces liver infection.

Choosing a good tomato can be tricky, especially in those stores where most tomatoes are already prepackaged when you buy them. A good one should be heavy in hand and smell slightly green, and its skin should be tight and spotless.

My favorite kind is the plain tomato, which is available from July until October. It is actually the very best variety for a fresh tomato salad.

TOMATO

FRESH TOMATO PULP

Serves 4

2¼ lb. tomatoes

1 bunch fresh tarragon

4 tablespoons sherry vinegar

Salt & pepper

1 tablespoon brown sugar

½ cup extra-virgin olive oil

Difficulty level: easy
Calories: 40
Preparation time: 4 hours

Remove the skin of the tomatoes after immersing them for 10 seconds in boiling water.

Chop the tomatoes very thinly until they become almost liquid.

Pass them through a cheesecloth and squeeze. Drain the pulp for 3 hours until it is almost completely dry.

Meanwhile, wash and dry the tarragon leaves. Chop them and keep them to one side.

Put the drained pulp in a bowl and add a splash of the vinegar, salt, pepper, sugar, olive oil, and tarragon. Mix the sauce with a fork and serve it at room temperature.

Delicious with toasted slices of baguette.

TOMATO CONFIT *(Pictured)*

Difficulty level: medium
Calories: 50
Preparation time: 1½ hours

Serves 6

2¼ lb. tomatoes

4 tablespoons honey

Salt & pepper

½ bunch fresh thyme

4 cloves garlic, crushed

¾ cup extra-virgin olive oil

Preheat the oven to 250°F.

Remove the skins of the tomatoes as above. Cut the tomatoes into quarters. Remove their pulp, making sure not to leave any seeds.

Dry them individually with a clean dish towel.

Put them on a baking sheet. Brush them on both sides with a mixture of honey, salt, pepper, fresh thyme, crushed garlic, and olive oil.

Then put them in the oven with the door slightly open for 1 hour. The tomatoes should be fairly dry but with a small amount of moisture still remaining.

TOMATO

TOMATO JAM

Serves 4

Difficulty level: easy
Calories: 80
Preparation time: 4 hours

2¼ lb. late-season tomatoes

3½ tablespoons unsalted butter

3 tablespoons brown sugar

2 oz. pickled ginger (thinly chopped)

1 lemon (juiced)

1¼ cups water

Thickly chop the last tomatoes of the season and put aside.

In a large, hot pan, brown the butter, then throw in the tomatoes and stir vigorously for 3 minutes. Add the brown sugar and stir again.

Add the pickled ginger, the lemon juice, and a good amount of water.

Cook on a low heat for 3 hours. When the water has evaporated from the tomatoes and it looks like a jam, remove the pan and let it cool.

Serve cold with fresh oysters, toasted bread, or grilled eggplant, for example.

MUSTARD & TOMATO FEUILLETÉ *(Pictured)*

Difficulty level: medium
Calories: 220
Preparation time: 45 minutes

Serves 6

1 lb. 2oz. tomatoes

1 good-quality puff pastry

⅓ cup Dijon mustard

3 tablespoons grated Parmesan cheese

Fresh thyme

Pepper

Extra-virgin olive oil

My mother probably cut out this recipe from the food section of *Cosmopolitan* in the summer of 1978—it was featured on the front of our fridge for years afterward. It is the most simple and delicious tomato recipe that has ever been invented.

Preheat the oven to 350°F.

Remove the stem of each tomato. Cut them into slices ⅛ inch thick.

Roll out the puff pastry and spread the mustard generously. Place the tomatoes over it and sprinkle over the Parmesan cheese, thyme, and pepper.

Cook in the hot oven for 12 minutes, then finish cooking the tart for another 3 minutes with the oven door slightly open so the humidity can evaporate.

Add a splash of olive oil just before serving.

TRUFFLE

One may think that because of its rarity and high cost, black truffle is a very special ingredient. Black truffle is no caviar. Black truffle is an aroma, a penetrating aroma. There is no folklore or anything mystical about it, but it is truly a special ingredient.

What makes this ingredient so special is the fact that you can't really learn how to use it. It takes years of practice and experimentation to start recognizing its qualities and using it judiciously.

You can buy black truffle in a tin, in purée, infused in oil, and of course fresh. You can infuse it, cook it, and add it to a mixture, but over the years, I have found that raw truffle is really the best.

It doesn't usually get interfered with by other ingredients and always brings a depth of aroma that complements the flavor of what it is mixed with.

So if you are still convinced that truffle is merely an expensive oddity, try the simple black truffle polenta.

SUMMER TRUFFLE RISOTTO

Difficulty level: hard
Calories: 345
Preparation time: 30 minutes

Serves 4

½ onion

9 oz. Carnaroli rice

1 cup extra-virgin olive oil

¼ cup white wine

2 cups chicken broth (page 32)

3½ tablespoons unsalted butter

¼ cup grated Parmesan cheese

2½ oz. mascarpone

2 tablespoons heavy cream
(optional)

¼ cup truffle oil

Salt & white pepper

½ cup chicken jus (page 29)

1½ oz. summer truffle

Chop the onion, fry it with the rice in half of the olive oil without browning, then add the wine and allow to evaporate until almost dry. Slowly add the chicken broth and cook for 14 minutes while stirring regularly.

Add the butter little by little, some of the Parmesan cheese, the mascarpone, and the remaining olive oil. Make sure the consistency is oily. If too hard, add a spoonful of whisked cream. Finish with truffle oil.

Add salt and pepper as needed.

Divide the risotto among 4 soup plates and pour over some warmed chicken jus. Finish by covering the risotto with some thinly sliced black truffle.

BLACK TRUFFLE POLENTA

Difficulty level: medium
Calories: 235
Preparation time: 40 minutes

Serves 4

½ cup extra-virgin olive oil

2 oz. celery (cut into small cubes)

2 oz. pumpkin (peeled, seeded & cut into small cubes)

4 oz. coarse cornmeal polenta

½ cup dry white wine

4 cups chicken broth (page 32)

1 oz. mascarpone

2 savoy cabbage leaves (boiled for 2 minutes & cut into small cubes)

3 tablespoons grated Parmesan cheese

Salt & pepper

¾ oz. black Perigord truffle

Into a large pot on a high heat add 1 tablespoon of olive oil until hot. Add in the celery and pumpkin and stir, making sure not to brown. Add the polenta and continue stirring on a low heat. Add the wine and reduce until almost dry.

Add the chicken broth gradually, and slowly and constantly stir using the handle of a wooden spoon. It helps break down polenta.

Cook for another 6 minutes, until the polenta starts thickening and is not swimming in the broth. Add the mascarpone and continue cooking at a low heat. Add the savoy cabbage and the Parmesan cheese. Finish by adding the remaining olive oil. By then the mixture should have a not-too-thick creamy texture.

Add the salt and pepper and divide the polenta among 4 soup plates. Slice the fresh truffle over each plate and serve immediately.

LATE-SUMMER TRUFFLE

Simmered autumn vegetables

Difficulty level: hard
Calories: 110
Preparation time: 45 minutes

Serves 4

2 tablespoons unsalted butter

2½ oz. celeriac (diced)

2½ oz. carrot (diced)

Salt & pepper

2 oz. parsnip (diced)

2 oz. leek (diced)

2 oz. white potato (diced)

**1 fresh summer truffle
(around 1 oz.)**

½ cup dry white wine

1 cup chicken broth (page 32)

Melt the butter and when it starts foaming, add the celeriac and carrot. Add a pinch of salt and stir on a very low heat. After 2 minutes, add the parsnip, leek, and potatoes. Stir for another 2 minutes while making sure that nothing sticks to the bottom of the pan. Add another small pinch of salt.

Add a bit of chopped black truffle and pour in the white wine. Reduce the white wine until it is almost dry and add the chicken broth. Bring to a simmer and cover. Cook for 7 minutes.

Check every 2 to 3 minutes to ensure that the heat is not excessive.

Once the vegetables are meltingly soft but not mushy, remove them from the heat and spoon them out into soup plates.

Add a little pepper to each plate and thinly slice the summer truffle over. Eat right away.

TURNIP

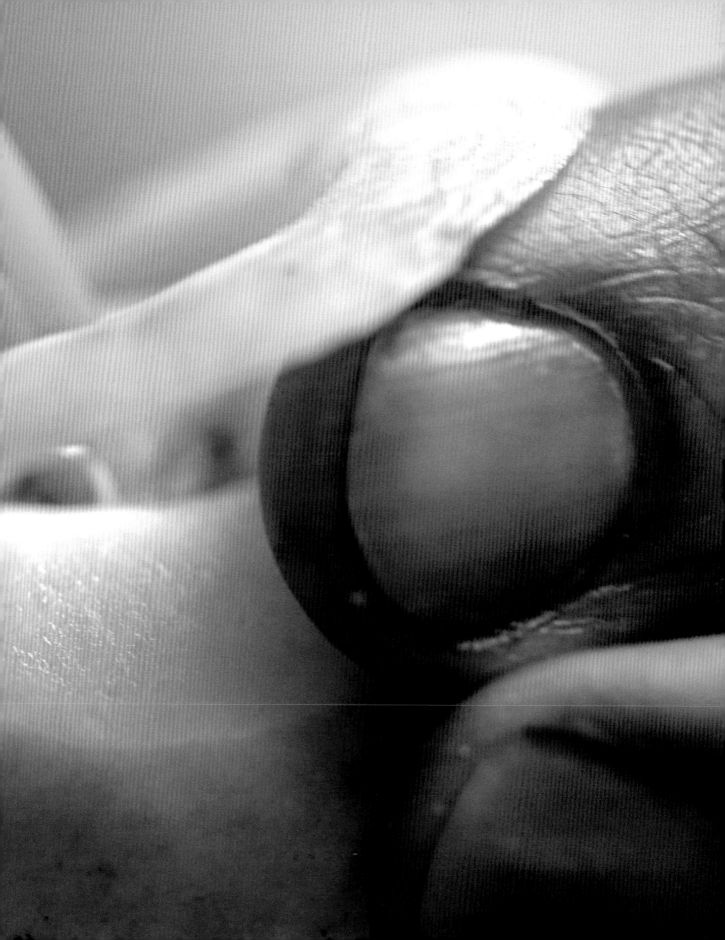

TURNIPS APICIUS

Difficulty level: hard
Calories: 180
Preparation time: 45 minutes

Among the most famous French dishes that I had to learn by heart when I was doing my apprenticeship, was the famous "Duck Apicius." Apicius was a gourmet during first-century Rome who wrote a book about condiments. One of the best was his famous mix of spices, honey and mint. A mix made in heaven.

The French rub duck breast with the Apicius blend to enhance the original flavor of the animal. So in my quest to attach new flavors to otherwise uninspiring vegetables, I first cooked turnips in honey, and thought that it tasted delicious. Then I thought of honey mixed with light spices and the Apicius mix came to my mind. Suddenly, turnips became as glorious as a duck breast.

Serves 4

2 bunches small round turnips (around 30)

¼ cup extra-virgin olive oil

Salt

1 tablespoon granulated sugar

4 cups chicken broth (page 32)

16 seedless grapes (halved)

3½ tablespoons unsalted butter

3 Granny Smith apples

Apicius mix

2 tablespoons honey

½ oz. coriander seeds

½ oz. fennel seeds

½ oz. white pepper

½ oz. cumin seeds

2 tablespoons dry white wine

2 mint leaves

Separate the turnips from their stems, retaining 1 inch attached.

Peel each turnip twice and keep them in cold water. Keep in the fridge for 30 minutes so they get very cold.

Start preparing the apicius mix by heating up the honey, coriander seeds, fennel seeds, pepper, and cumin seeds together in a pan on a very low heat. When the seeds start caramelizing, add the wine and mint leaves.

Let it simmer slowly until it starts thickening. Make sure to brush the sides of the pan from time to time so it doesn't burn.

When the apicius mix starts looking like a thick honey, remove from the heat and keep at room temperature.

Pour some olive oil into a large pan on high heat. When the oil starts smoking, add the turnips and stir for 20 seconds. Add salt and sugar. Add the chicken broth and cover. It should take 5 minutes for the turnips to reach a meltingly soft texture.

Add the grapes to the turnips and cook for another 3 minutes. Add 2 spoonfuls of the apicius mix and let the liquid evaporate.

Remove the pan when the turnips and grapes start caramelizing. Lay them on a plate, alternating the grapes and turnips. Put the pan back on a high heat and add another spoonful of apicius mix together with the butter. The butter will create a sauce with the apicius mix.

Pour this sauce over the turnips and grapes and add some very thinly sliced Granny Smith apples.

BITTER SLICES OF RAW TURNIP
Tuna & wasabi mayonnaise

Difficulty level: medium
Calories: 150
Preparation time: 30 minutes

This simple salad is all about texture. The crunchy, bitter slices of tiny turnips bring texture to a soft and creamy slice of fatty tuna. The whole thing comes together in the rich wasabi mayonnaise that glues everything together. The turnip leaves bring a bit of refreshment to the combination without taking over the original texture and flavor. A simple, well-constructed, and seriously impressive salad.

Serves 4

- 3 oz. small turnips (with their leaves)
- 1 egg yolk
- 1 tablespoon sweet soy sauce
- 1 teaspoon wasabi
- ¾ cup sunflower oil
- Salt & white pepper
- 2 limes (juiced)
- 6 oz. toro (fatty) tuna loin (trimmed and then frozen)

Remove the greenest turnip leaves and wash them under cold water. Dry them with a clean dish towel and store them in the fridge.

Wash and peel the turnips. Keep them in icy water. Slice them very thinly with a Japanese mandoline (or a very sharp knife if you don't have one) and put them in ice. They will become crunchier.

In a bowl, whisk the egg yolk and soy sauce with the wasabi and slowly add the sunflower oil. Continue whisking until it becomes the texture of a liquid mayonnaise. Add a pinch of salt, the juice of one lime, and some white pepper.

Remove the tuna from the freezer and cut some thin slices with a long knife.

In a bowl, season the crunchy slices of turnips with the mayonnaise.

On 4 large plates, alternate the slices of toro tuna with the slices of turnips and the fresh turnip leaves. Finish by pouring over the juice of the other lime with some salt and pepper.

ZUCCHINI

The zucchini is very easy to digest and contains only 17 calories for every 3 ounces eaten. It is super rich in water and potassium and very low in sodium. I have heard people say that it is a very calming vegetable and it is sometimes administered as a cure for hyperactive kids!

When I was working in California as a private chef, I was able to pick some vegetables from the garden behind the house. My favorite ingredient was the zucchini blossom.

Catherina, the garden boss, couldn't understand why I was removing the flowers of her zucchini. What was the point? she always asked me.

I just wanted to stuff them or to mix them in a salad.

We were in the early 1990s and this was a sort of nouvelle cuisine that she couldn't understand. The zucchini blossom is now very expensive, and quite popular. If you feel like having some, I would recommend eating them raw in salad, because stuffing the zucchini blossom is probably the single item that represents for me what nouvelle cuisine was all about.

Times are changing and zucchini is now eaten early in its season as a vegetable rather than as a flower. So that is good.

In order to recognize a good zucchini, you need to make sure that it is heavy and the skin is thin, shiny, and spotless. It can be small, long, round, short, or even twisted. A good zucchini, just like a tomato, should feel heavy in hand to taste good.

MARINATED ZUCCHINI & LIME
Scallops and jalapeño pepper

Difficulty level: medium
Calories: 85
Preparation time: 2 hours 30 minutes

Zucchini is just like your most boring friend. An absolute bore when on his/her own! But as soon as you add a combination of texture, flavor, and presentation, it suddenly turns into the perfect partner. Zucchini are not going to change your life, but they will definitely become part of it. This dish is the perfect example.

Serves 4

- 2 large zucchini
- 2 limes (juiced)
- Salt & pepper
- 10 tablespoons extra-virgin olive oil
- ½ shallot
- ½ clove garlic
- ¼ red pepper
- ¼ tiny jalapeño pepper
- ½ lemon (juiced)
- 2 tablespoons white wine vinegar
- 1 tablespoon soy sauce
- 4 scallops

For the zucchini

Wash the zucchini and slice as thinly as you can (about ⅛ inch thick) with a very sharp, long knife (so the zucchini won't crack or break).

Put the slices in a bowl with the juice of one lime, salt, pepper, and 4 tablespoons of olive oil.

Cover the bowl with plastic wrap and refrigerate for at least 2 hours.

Making the marinade

Chop the shallot, garlic clove, red pepper, and jalapeño pepper into tiny little cubes and put them in a medium bowl.

Add the juice of the other lime and half a lemon. Add the white wine vinegar, soy sauce, the remaining olive oil, salt, and black pepper and stir.

Slice the scallops flat, the same thickness as the zucchini.

On a large round plate, make a zucchini rosette, alternating with smaller rosettes of thinly sliced scallops.

Pour the marinade over and serve.

ZUCCHINI & MINT GRANITA

Difficulty level: medium
Calories: 80 calories
Preparation time: 3 hours

My kids categorically refused to be fed zucchini. Nothing I could do. I tried to hide it everywhere: in purée under a steak, mixed in soup with mint, mixed with rice ... I even attempted the unforgivable: a zucchini pizza! Nothing ever worked until I decided to try it with sweet things. Suddenly I realized that zucchini could give some sort of body to a simple granita or sorbet. I tried and it worked. So now when I am asked if my kids eat everything, I proudly say YES! Even zucchini!

Serves 4

1½ lb. zucchini

1 bunch Corsican mint (or common mint if you can't get Corsican)

1 lime (juiced)

½ cup sugar

2 cups water

Wash the zucchini and remove both ends. Grate the zucchini skins against a cheese grater. Keep the grated skins in a bowl (I know it will look really mashed!) and chop the rest of the zucchini in a food processor with the mint leaves. This will turn into a bright-green lumpy juice.

Put the lime juice in a saucepan and add the sugar and the water. Bring it to a boil and let it cool. When the mixture is almost cold, add the mashed green skin and put in the freezer.

Scratch the top of the ice with a fork every 2 hours in order to get a perfect granita.

You can serve it as a starter or a pudding with a splash of lime juice.

OVEN-BAKED ZUCCHINI

Confit tomatoes

Difficulty level: easy
Calories: 90
Preparation time: 90 minutes

After many years of eating and cooking watery vegetables, I can happily say that when they are simply cooked with olive oil in a pot they are absolutely wonderful. But the moment they are finished with a bit of thyme and Parmesan cheese they take on another dimension. Their original flavor is suddenly enhanced. It is like watching a film in 2D and suddenly seeing it in 3D. Sense-popping!

Serves 4

- 1¾ lb. ripe plum tomatoes
- 3 tablespoons extra-virgin olive oil
- 1 clove garlic
- Salt & pepper
- 1 tablespoon sugar
- 4 sprigs fresh thyme (lemon thyme can also be used)
- 1¼ lb. zucchini (fattest you can find)
- 2 tablespoons grated Parmesan cheese

Preheat the oven to 250°F.

Remove the stem of each tomato and wash them under very cold water for 20 seconds. Drain and dry. Cut them in ⅛-inch-thick slices.

Put 1 tablespoon olive oil in a large roasting pan and rub the garlic clove over it.

Line slices of tomato in the pan and add salt, pepper, sugar, and a little fresh thyme.

Sprinkle on 1 tablespoon of olive oil and put in the oven for 10 minutes.

After 10 minutes, open the oven door slightly—you can use a wooden spoon to prevent the door from closing fully. Let the tomatoes dehydrate and concentrate their taste for a further 30 minutes.

Meanwhile, wash the zucchini and cut them into ⅛-inch-thick slices.

Put them in a medium bowl and toss in 1 tablespoon olive oil with salt and pepper.

When the tomatoes are ready, alternate them with the zucchini in a pot. Sprinkle over the Parmesan cheese and the remaining thyme.

Put the oven to broil and finish with a little grilling of the Parmesan cheese and thyme tops.

Serve very hot. You will be amazed by the smell of thyme, Parmesan, and tomato gratin. So memorable!

ZUCCHINI, EGGPLANT, & SAFFRON CREAM

Difficulty level: medium
Calories: 150
Preparation time: 30 minutes

Some ingredients just seem to always work when they are paired together. They usually complement each other because of the contrast they apply: tomato and onion, artichoke and truffle, basil and garlic, brown butter and lemon . . . One of the weirdest perfect combinations is the one between zucchini and eggplant. Bluntly speaking, they are two weak vegetables. A bit too watery to balance each other, you would think. It just goes to show that vegetables are unpredictable and we should never assume anything.

Serves 4

- 1 lb. 2 oz. zucchini
- 1 lb. 2 oz. eggplant
- 1 red bell pepper
- Extra-virgin olive oil
- Salt & pepper
- 1 tablespoon superfine sugar
- 2 cups heavy cream
- ¼ teaspoon saffron
- 11 oz. water

Wash and cut the zucchini, eggplant, and red pepper into small cubes.

Pour some olive oil into a large flat pan and fry the cubes, making sure to stir vigorously so they don't burn at the base of the pan. Add salt, pepper, and sugar.

Continue stirring until the cubes start caramelizing. Add the cream and saffron. Stir and add water.

Cover and cook at a slow simmer for 10 minutes.

Do not drain. Liquidize the soup so it turns creamy.

Add more salt and pepper as needed, and serve very hot with a dollop of cream and a few saffron strands.

BECOMING A HAIRDRESSER

It is common knowledge that kitchens are not reknowned for refined and distinguished conversation. It is usually somewhere that pretty much everyone swears, shouts, abuses, and sometimes hits one another.

Having spent too many years working in kitchens, I could write an entire book about capricious, inflated, egocentric chefs who commonly abuse their staff.

So when I reached the highlight of my apprenticeship by working in a 3-Michelin-star kitchen, I knew that I would have to suffer many insults . . . and I was ready for that. What I wasn't ready for was a question my head chef would ask me, day in day out, for over two years: Why don't you become a hairdresser?

From the moment I entered the kitchen until the moment I left at night, I was subjected to the most terrible harassment one can imagine. He would constantly question my desire to become a chef. And the question wasn't naïve at all. Being a hairdresser is the complete opposite of the macho image a chef has to have.

So glad was I at not having followed his cheap career advice that I married a hairdresser!

FRUITS

Like a new partner, a fruit needs to be touched to tell you how good it is going to be. Fruit is an obsession for me. I am fascinated by its diversity and how it impacts one's life. Everyone has a favorite fruit, and you can always tell a lot about someone by the fruit he or she prefers. Tell me what fruit you love and I will tell you who you are.

My uncle Henry, who pretty much brought me up, was the king of fruit at home. Not surprising, since he was chief trader for the Avignon fruit market! He lived his life around fruit, its qualities, and its prices.

He loved talking about them and talking to them, and he naturally loved eating them. He was so much into his fruit that he slowly developed fruit shapes in his body. His face was as round as a tangerine, his arms were like two bananas, his legs were as strong as pineapples, and his chest was like a big grapefruit.

He respected fruit and understood it like nobody else. He would also always try to find a good excuse when a fruit was not so good: maybe the weather, maybe the producer, but never the fruit itself. As far as he was concerned, fruit was always perfect. No matter its shape or its color.

I believed every word he said, until I started traveling!

When I first arrived in California in 1995, I was taken to Stanford shopping center in Palo Alto, where I was told that I could find the very best seasonal fruits. We were there in mid-December and I imagined I would find the same sort of fruit I could find in any south-of-France market, since the weather was quite similar—the softest persimmon, the shiniest dates, the first oranges of the season, and the sharpest lemons.

In fact, I found myself looking at beautifully arranged rows of imported cherries, uniform raspberries, plenty of exotic fruit, and for each fruit a picture of the farmer smiling happily in the middle of his field. What the hell, I thought. Fruit was no longer a marker of the season we were in. I can't describe the precise feeling I had on that December day. Fruit was lost, and I was lost.

(cont.)

Then I saw a massive strawberry. I had been cheated, the fruit had been cheated, and I was supposed to find amazing the sight of a 4½-pound bloated strawberry. Even more annoying was being told that I could keep it for at least 3 weeks and could feed up to 10 adults with it.

Suddenly fruit had lost their promise.

I decided to venture out to find some persimmon to purchase. Sadly, they had been wrapped in a packet of two and below the cheesy picture of the smiling farmer was written in capital letters:

DO NOT TOUCH THE FRUIT.

What? Was I supposed to imagine what they would taste like in my mouth without feeling their skin under my fingers? Exactly so!

It became very stressful. I had spent more than twenty years developing my understanding of fruit by touching it, smelling it, and pressing it before putting it in my mouth, and here I was trying to spot the one with the darkest color and the shiniest skin. I picked up a packet of two—one of them was great, the other one was too hard and not ready to be eaten.

Silly me, I should have known; I should have recognized the perfect one, the one next to this one maybe. But I couldn't: my hands, which are supposed to help me choose, had to stay away from the fruit.

It is like going to a museum and being asked not to touch the art. Frustrating! I don't want to be frustrated, I want to use my hands. I want to use all of my senses.

From that day, I promised myself that I would never buy any fruit I hadn't touched or smelled beforehand.

APPLE

An apple a day keeps the doctor away. We have all been told this.

Actually, it is not one but three a day that we should be eating. Three apples a day for 45 days is said to reduce your cholesterol by between 10 percent and 40 percent. In order to achieve this you have to eat the apple unpeeled; otherwise it will take a little bit longer to work. I should actually be writing about the pectin instead of the apple. Pectin is very good for slowing the process of absorbing sugar into the blood. It protects our pancreas while reducing our intake of insulin.

We all need to eat apples; it's best to have them at the beginning of each meal. It will help your system digest sugar and fat more easily.

There are many kinds of apples available and it is sometimes quite hard to find the one that is going to work best with what you are going to make. The following pages will indicate the guidelines I follow.

APPLE

DEEP-FRIED: SWEET APPLE TEMPURA

Serves 4

Difficulty level: medium
Calories: 280
Preparation time: 45 minutes

3 oz. tempura mix (you can find this in your international supermarket aisle)

½ cup very cold water

2¼ lb. apples, such as Melrose or Jonagold

2 cups sunflower oil

Confectioners' sugar

In a bowl, mix the tempura powder with the water. Whisk until you get a thin, creamy paste free of any lumps.

Peel and core the apples. Cut them into any shape as long as they are all of the same thickness of around ¼ inch.

Heat some sunflower oil to 400°F. Drop a touch of tempura mix into the oil when you feel it is hot enough. If the tempura sets and start frying, your oil is ready.

Coat the apple in the tempura mix and cook in the hot oil, turning the pieces of apple over after 2 minutes. Remove them from the hot oil and drain them on a cloth. Sprinkle on some confectioners' sugar and serve.

OVEN-ROASTED: POMEGRANATE ROASTED APPLE *(Pictured)*

Serves 4

Difficulty level: medium
Calories: 324
Preparation time: 30 minutes

8 Golden Delicious apples

½ stick (4 tablespoons) unsalted butter (cut into small cubes)

8 tablespoons honey

8 tablespoons pomegranate syrup

2 fresh pomegranate (seeds)

Preheat the oven to 350°F. Clean the apples but do not peel. Core and remove all the seeds.

Lay the apples in a buttered roasting pan. Put a spoonful of butter in the middle of each apple, add a spoonful of honey, a spoonful of pomegranate syrup, and some pomegranate seeds.

Bake for 10 minutes. Serve immediately.

APPLE

BAKED

Diffficulty level: easy
Calories: 155
Preparation time: 1 hour 30 minutes Marinating: 12 hours

Serves 4

- 2 oranges (juiced)
- 3 oz. glass sweet white wine (preferably Riesling)
- 2 tablespoons brown sugar
- 1 teaspoon cinnamon
- 1 teaspoon ground cloves
- 1 teaspoon ground ginger
- 1 teaspoon ground aniseed
- 10 Pippin apples (peeled, cored & cut into halves)
- Crème fraîche

If you feel like baking apples, I really recommend using Pippin.

In a bowl, put the orange juice, Riesling, sugar, and spices. Add the apples and let them marinate for 12 hours. Put the apples in a baking pan and put in the oven at 425°F for 1 hour. Remove from the oven and put in a bowl. Smash the apples gently with a wooden spoon and mix in the juice left in the oven dish.

Serve at room temperature topped with crème fraîche.

CARAWAY & APPLE COMPOTE *(Pictured)*

Difficulty level: easy
Calories: 165
Preparation time: 45 minutes

Serves 4

- 2¼ lb. Golden Delicious apple
- ½ stick (4 tablespoons) unsalted butter
- ½ cup superfine sugar
- 2 teaspoon crushed caraway seeds
- ½ cup dry white wine
- 1 cup water

Always use very ripe fruit. You must also use the most flavorful apples available, such as Elstar or Golden Delicious.

Peel and cut the apples into 8. Remove any hard parts and make sure to remove any seeds. Wash under cold water. Melt the butter in a thick-bottomed pan and add the apple. Stir and add the sugar. Continue stirring until the sugar looks like it has melted. Add the caraway seeds and the white wine.

Reduce the wine until it has almost completely evaporated and add the water. Cover and cook at a very slow simmer for 12 minutes.

The apples should have turned mushy. Break them even more with a spoon while making sure that the remaining liquid evaporates. Refrigerate and serve very cold. Delicious when mixed with yogurt.

RAW APPLE

Beef & Jonagold carpaccio

Difficulty level: medium
Calories: 120
Preparation time: 10 minutes

I love raw apple with my meat. I think that beef and raw apple are meant to be served together. Thinly sliced apple on top of raw beef carpaccio is delicious. The best apples for this purpose are the Jonagold or Boskoop. They are tightly fibered, a little acidic, and very juicy.

Serves 4

- 9 oz. beef filet
- 8 Jonagold apples
- 1 lemon (juiced)
- ½ pink shallot
- ½ cup olive oil
- ¼ cup balsamic vinegar
- Salt & pepper

Cut the beef filet into very thin slices and divide among 4 large plates. Peel and core the apples. Slice them very thinly and pour a little lemon juice over them.

Slice the shallot very thinly and divide it among the 4 plates. Add the olive oil, vinegar, salt, and pepper.

Do not wait too long to serve this dish once it is ready, as the apples will very quickly turn dark and the vinegar will start cooking the beef.

FAT DUCK APPLE

Difficulty level: medium
Calories: 230
Preparation time: 45 minutes

Apple and foie gras have always been a match made in heaven. The richness of the foie gras married with the slight acidity of the apple is a perfect balance. It is almost like a man and a woman. Adam and Eve! Here, for once, the apple is on top.

Serves 4

- 4 Royal Gala apples
- Salt
- ¼ cup olive oil, plus more for pan
- ¾ cup port
- 2 tablespoons honey
- 2 white onions
- 4 slices duck foie gras (2 oz. each or ½ inch thick)
- 2 sprigs thyme
- 1 sprig parsley (chopped)

Wash the apples and cut them width-wise in 2. Remove the stem, making sure you don't break the apple.

Boil the apples in a little salted water for 3 minutes. Remove and lay the apples on an oiled baking sheet.

Cook in the oven with the door ajar at 325°F for 25 minutes, until the apples are soft but not mushy.

In a pan, boil the port together with the honey until reduced to a thick consistency.

Peel and thinly slice the onions. Slowly cook in a pan with the olive oil, while almost constantly stirring, until the onions are soft and slightly brown.

Remove the onions from the pan and in the same pan, fry the slices of foie gras after salting them on both sides. The heat must be very strong so the fois gras is seared rather than boiled. Cook the foie gras for 1 minute on each side and remove.

Once the apples are ready, reconstruct the apple by putting the bottom half of the apple at the bottom, topped with the foie gras, onion, and the top half of the apple—just like a burger in its bun.

Add a little fresh thyme and chopped parsley, and re-create the stem of the apple with some parsley stalks. Pour the reduction of port and honey over each apple.

GRANNY'S SORBET

Granny Smith & black sesame seeds

Difficulty level: easy
Calories: 120
Preparation time: 3½ hours

Serves 8

- ¾ oz. black sesame seeds
- ¾ cup water
- 1 cup granulated sugar
- 1 teaspoon pectin powder
- 4 cups Granny Smith apple juice
- 1 lemon (juiced)

Set the oven to broil and slightly toast the sesame seeds.

Start by bringing the water and sugar to a boil.

Add the sesame seeds.

Add the pectin powder and chill for 3 hours.

Add the apple juice and the lemon juice.

Turn in an ice-cream machine.

If you don't have an ice-cream machine, you can freeze the mixture and scratch it with a fork as it becomes frozen. It will turn into a delicious granita.

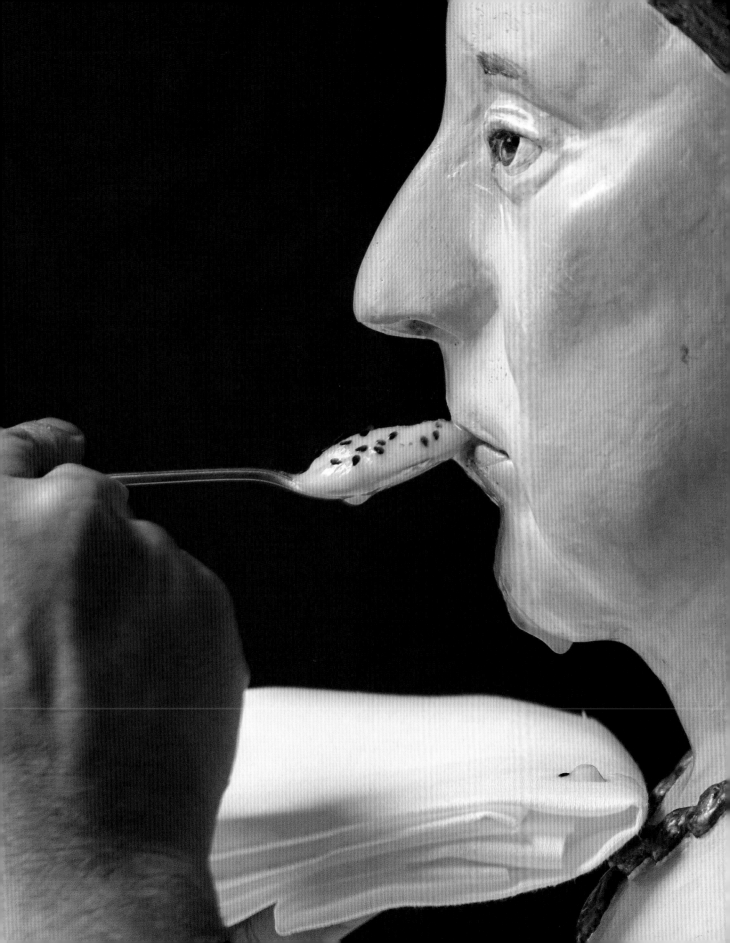

APRICOT

It is funny how an apricot transforms itself during its exposure to the sun.

It can be eaten very early in the season (say, mid-June) for those who love acidity, or can be eaten very late (end of August).

What I really love about apricots is that it is never too late or too early in the season to enjoy them.

The apricot is very familiar to me. The south of France is a large producer of apricots and I can remember them being part of our meals throughout the summer.

It is quite hard to find a perfect apricot, and we should always bite into it before deciding what to do with it. It is not rare to find some beautiful-looking apricots that taste too ripe or too acidic, or whose flesh is too white (even though their skin is deep orange).

An acidic apricot is great when poached in syrup or prepared as a crumble with lots of sugar.

A freshly picked apricot (tight skin, tender flesh, and perfect balance of sweet and acidity) is only good when eaten raw and on its own.

And when they are very ripe, it is usually best to make them into jam. Is there a better summery jam than an apricot one? No way.

APRICOT

ACIDIC EARLY-SEASON APRICOT CRUMBLE

Difficulty level: medium
Calories: 450
Preparation time: 1 hour

Serves 4

7 tablespoons unsalted butter

1 cup superfine sugar

2 oz. ground almonds

16 apricots (keep the apricot pits, as they can be really useful in a kitchen; see below), cut in half

3 eggs

Pinch of salt

2 tablespoons rum

½ cup all-purpose flour

Brown sugar

¾ cup cream

In a large, hot pan, brown half the butter. Add half of the sugar, the ground almonds, and the apricots. Toss them for 3 to 4 minutes and put on a very low heat. Cover with a lid. You may have to add half a glass of water if it starts getting too dry.

Meanwhile mix the eggs, the remaining butter, sugar, salt, rum, and flour together until you get a crumbly dough.

When the apricots are cooked, remove them from the pot and let them cool.

Lay the apricots in a large dish, making sure to pour the cooking jus over.

Break the crumble over them, covering up to ½ inch thick. Sprinkle some brown sugar over it. The dough should be ½ inch high on top of the apricots. Cook in an oven at 350°F for 7 minutes in grill position.

Serve warm with some cream on the side.

APRICOT GRANITA *(Pictured)*

Difficulty level: easy
Calories: 300
Preparation time: 6 hours

Serves 4

4 cups water

¾ cup sugar

20 apricot pits

9 oz. shrimp (cooked & peeled)

1½ oz. crushed peanuts

2 tablespoons extra-virgin olive oil

Pepper

I hope that you kept every single apricot pit you were ready to throw away.

When the apricot season ends, I sometimes find myself craving the fruit's flavor. That is when I infuse the apricot pits in syrup and make a granita out of it. It is extremely simple, yet it has a wonderful depth of flavor.

Boil the water and the sugar together. Add the apricot pits and let them infuse until cold, then place in the freezer. Scratch the surface of the frozen apricot syrup with a fork every hour for about 5 hours.

In a frozen martini glass, put a third of the granita. Top with some shrimp and sprinkle some crushed peanuts. Add a dash of olive oil and some freshly ground black pepper.

Serve as a starter.

APRICOT, CHICKPEAS & CILANTRO

Difficulty level: medium
Calories: 140
Preparation time: 30 minutes

Serves 4

- **2 tablespoons unsalted butter**
- **12 apricots, cut in half**
- **4 oz. cooked chickpeas**
- **1½ oz. shallots (chopped)**
- **¼ cup extra-virgin olive oil**
- **2 tablespoons white wine vinegar**
- **Salt & pepper**
- **½ bunch cilantro (chopped)**
- **½ cup bran flakes (available in your cereal aisle)**

Slowly warm the butter in a pan until it turns brown. Add the apricots and gently cook them until the skin starts detaching itself and the apricot turns mushy. Slowly stir for 5 minutes and remove from the heat. Let the apricots cool.

In a large vegetable bowl, mix together the chickpeas, shallots, olive oil, vinegar, salt, and pepper.

Gently add the apricots, making sure not to break them too much. The flesh must keep a little bit of texture.

Serve in a soup plate and add the chopped cilantro and sprinkle over some bran flakes.

AVOCADO

When I left France in 1995, and after spending many years in gastronomic restaurants covered in Michelin stars, I had absolutely no idea that you could actually do something with avocado.

Avocados were invisible in the restaurants where I had worked. If you wanted to be taken seriously, you could not have avocado on your menu. That was the norm.

One of the worst insults I was subjected to, when at Ducasse, was to be told that I was only good to cook avocado. Obviously, that would make the entire brigade laugh and would make me look very small, and the head chef very big. Not a nice man, but I've touched on that before.

Don't get me wrong, I had eaten avocado at home in the '80s; my mother sometimes served it. She would simply prepare it with a classic vinaigrette as a starter, but that was it.

Avocado was at this time the perfect example of food you would find at a roadside restaurant—served with tiny shrimp and shredded lettuce and covered in cocktail sauce. Back then no combination with another ingredient had transformed or enhanced this fruit.

So when I started working as a private chef in San Francisco in September 1995 my boss, who had been brought up on delicious California avocado, asked me to prepare some. I wanted to impress him: I wanted to show him that I was a creative and talented young French chef who could transform anything into something exceptional. So I decided to cook the most disgusting thing I have ever done: hot avocado flan. It was worse than anything one could imagine. It was extremely bitter and weird in texture with a horrible gray-blue colour. But being French and proud (and stupid), I decided to serve it. My boss was very forgiving and accepted my apology on the basis that avocado was an exotic product for me. I went through a long and delicious educational process after that, which opened many of my closed brain cells!

During the avocado season, which lasts from November to May, I love mixing them with fresh citrus fruit, marinated fatty fish, and even crispy duck skin. I still love my avocado vinaigrette, but there are so many other wonderful things you can do with avocado that it is a pity to just stop there.

To be good, an avocado has to be ripe. I have learned over the years to be patient in order to get the perfect texture. It is a difficult act to balance as sometimes a day or two can make all the difference. When I look for the best avocado, I usually buy only the ones you can touch. I need to weigh them in my hand. If they feel heavy, have very shiny skins, and are free of any stains, these are usually good signs. Then I usually check at the base if the stem is very fixed or starts moving a bit. Then I slightly press on its skin, making sure not to break it. If there is a slight light resistance, it probably means that the avocado is soon going to be perfect. I double-check by slightly shaking the fruit. If I feel that the pit is moving a little bit, it means it is ripe. That is the one I buy.

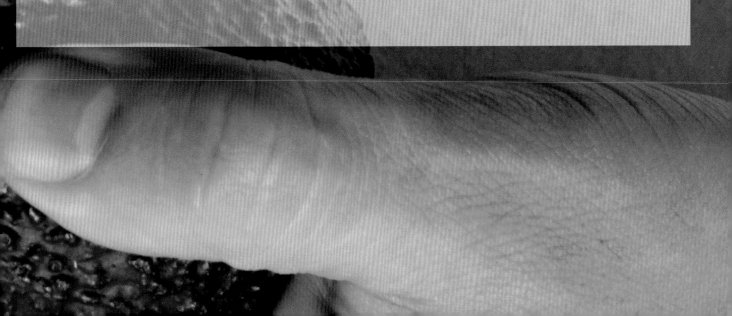

AVOCADO & QUINOA SALAD

Pink grapefruit, mint & fennel

Difficulty level: medium
Calories: 385
Preparation time: 40 minutes

Serves 4

- 2 pink grapefruits
- 3 tablespoons sherry vinegar
- 1 tablespoon Dijon mustard
- ½ cup extra-virgin olive oil
- Salt & pepper
- 4 baby fennel (washed & thinly sliced with a Japanese mandoline)
- 4 oz. quinoa (cooked for 8 minutes in boiling salted water, drained & refreshed)
- 20 mint leaves (washed & thinly chopped)
- 4 Hass avocados

Peel and segment the grapefruit, reserving 3 tablespoons of the juice for the dressing. In a large bowl start by preparing the dressing. Pour the grapefruit juice together with the vinegar. Add the mustard and whisk the mixture.

Add the olive oil, salt, pepper, the sliced fennel, the quinoa, and the mint leaves.

Stir and taste. Add salt if needed.

Open the avocados, remove their pits, and spoon them out from their skins. Slice them and divide them among 4 large plates. Place the quinoa mix and the grapefruit segments over them.

Add more chopped mint and serve.

AVOCADO, WATERCRESS & CELERY

Difficulty level: easy
Calories: 280
Preparation time: 40 minutes

Serves 4

- ¾ cup balsamic vinegar
- ½ cup water
- 1 tablespoon superfine sugar
- 1 head celery (cleaned & washed)
- 1 bunch watercress
- 4 Hass avocados
- 1 lemon (zest & juice)
- ¼ cup crème fraîche
- Salt & pepper

Start this recipe by reducing the balsamic vinegar, which is used at the end of this dish. In a thick-bottomed pan, reduce the balsamic vinegar with the water and the sugar by half.

The balsamic is going to get a little bit thicker and a lot more powerful. Leave it to cool.

Thinly slice the head of celery with a mandoline and keep the pieces in icy water for 30 minutes so they turn very crunchy. It is important that the celery gets this texture in order to balance the softness of the avocado in the finished dish.

Remove the leaves from the watercress and clean them. Dry them out and keep them in the fridge until just before serving.

Open the avocados and remove their pits. Put them on a cutting board and cut them into thin slices with a very sharp knife.

Divide them among 4 large plates. Put the crunchy celery (which you will have dried and quickly seasoned with the lemon juice) over them and cover with the cream. Add the watercress leaves and lemon zest, and spoon some dollops of the balsamic vinegar reduction.

Add some salt and pepper and serve immediately.

CHERRY

There was a tradition in my family around the middle of June: As soon as the cherries were ripe, we were sent to our friends who had some magnificent cherry trees and were told to climb on the trees and eat as much as we wanted. We were left alone for an entire afternoon and we used to eat so much that for the next 4 days we would have a tummy ache and we wouldn't dare eat any more for the rest of the season!

This way our parents were sure that we were not going to eat too many cherries through the season. It is well known that cherries are extremely high in sugar and therefore very bad for us!

What they probably didn't know is that the cherry usually relieves headaches and is also a natural antiseptic.

How can I be sure to find the best cherry? Despite the fact that I have been overeating cherries for many years, I am still very excited to see them come back in June.

I get very upset when I see them around Christmas when they are brought from Chile—even more annoying is the fact they are sometimes extremely good!

The first cherry I eat should be the template of what I expect for the rest of the season.

I enjoy waiting and choosing the one that is going to be the first to pop into my mouth. I have to enjoy my first cherry—but I want to have the best. I will wait until the moment I come across the one that is going to tell me: Eat me! I am the perfect one for you.

A dark color, a tight but slightly soft skin, shiny with some blurry reflections.

I take it into my fingers, I inspect it, I am very careful, I prepare my mouth to receive it, I send a message to my brain telling it to be prepared to taste the first cherry of the year. I put it in my mouth and press on its skin with my teeth. The skin should break firmly and release its juice through my teeth. I would then swallow the juice and palpate the texture left with my tongue. Suddenly I would feel the pit and make it roll on my tongue in order to remove the flesh that sticks on it.

I would swallow the flesh and breathe through my nose.

Then I would spit out the pit—don't swallow it!

The retro-olfaction of the cherry will fix the taste onto my brain and will remind me what the taste of a perfect cherry should be: dark, red, and juicy.

CHERRY

ROASTED CHERRIES WITH RIESLING *(Pictured)*

Difficulty level: easy
Calories: 205
Preparation time: 1 hour

Serves 4

¾ cup dry Riesling

1 teaspoon ground cinnamon

1 teaspoon ground ginger

½ cup brown sugar

1 orange (zest)

6 oz. cherries

¼ cup crème fraîche

Preheat the oven to 325°F.

Whisk the Riesling with the spices. Then add the sugar and continue whisking until the sugar has completely dissolved. Add the orange zest.

Tip the cherries onto a buttered baking sheet and cover them with the Riesling and spice mix. Cover with aluminum foil and cook for 30 minutes. Make sure you shake the sheet from time to time.

Serve either hot or cold with a large spoonful of crème fraîche over the cherries.

GRANDMA'S CHERRY CLAFOUTIS

Difficulty level: medium
Calories: 370
Preparation time: 1 hour

Serves 4

3 cups all-purpose flour

1¼ cups granulated sugar

Pinch salt

2 drops white wine vinegar

8 eggs

4 cups whole milk

½ cup heavy cream, plus more for serving

Butter, for greasing

2 handfuls overripe, unpitted (pits in!) cherries

2 teaspoons kirsch

Preheat the oven to 350°F. Put the flour, sugar, salt, and vinegar in a big bowl. Whisk them together and add the eggs one at a time. Pour in the milk and the cream while whisking.

Butter a large pie plate. Rinse the cherries and spread them all over the dish. Pour the mix over and put in the oven for 35 minutes.

Serve warm with a bit of kirsch and a spoonful of cream on each plate.

Remember that the cherries should be cooked with their pits in.

"I get very upset when I see cherries around Christmas when they are brought from Chile—even more annoying is the fact they are sometimes extremely good!"

JOLLY JELLY BABY

Raspberry & mint flavored jelly baby

Difficulty level: medium
Calories: 270
Preparation time:1 hours 30 minutes Freezing: 24 hours

Taste, texture, and, most important, shape are constantly on my mind when I try to inspire kids and get them interested in creating dishes. I recently found some amazing pastry molds made out of silicone. They are great for bringing a bit of creativity and sometimes eccentricity to what could otherwise be a boring dish. Get creative next time you're at your kitchen-supply store!

Serves 4

Raspberry jus

½ cup water

½ cup superfine sugar

14 oz. fresh raspberries

Jelly

¾ cup granulated sugar

2 cups water

½ cup mint syrup

9 gelatin sheets

2 teaspoons peppermint essence

For the raspberry jus

Boil the water together with the sugar. As soon as it boils, remove from the heat and let it cool. In a blender, blend the raspberries until liquified and add the cool syrup.

Place in the freezer and let it freeze for at least 5 hours. After 5 hours, try to stretch it into a long shape and put it back in the freezer for a minimum of 12 hours.

Making the jelly

Boil the sugar, water, and mint syrup together. Remove from the stove as soon as it boils and let it cool for 5 minutes.

Add the gelatin sheets and the peppermint essence and gently stir, making sure that the gelatin is well dissolved. Wait until the syrup is at room temperature and start filling the jelly baby mold. Only fill ¾ of its volume and let it almost set in the fridge for 2 hours.

Take it out of the fridge and place the frozen raspberry purée inside. Cover with the remaining unset mint jelly and keep in the fridge to finish setting for at least 8 hours.

Removing the jelly from the mold should not be too hard. However, if you experience difficulties, just set the mold in hot water for 30 seconds.

MARINATED FIGS IN SANGRIA

Difficulty level: medium
Calories: 285
Preparation time: 1 hour

The fig has always been a main part of my nutrition. We had a huge fig tree at our house in Avignon and I remember my mother endlessly preparing fig jam when the fruit was overripe. We just couldn't eat all the fruit. Figs can get so sweet that you almost don't have to add sugar to the jam. The figs get the sun during the whole summer—it is only in September that you can really appreciate them when they are dark and very soft.

Serves 4

Sangria

- **2 cups red wine**
- **⅓ cup granulated sugar**
- **1 orange (halved)**
- **1 lemon (halved)**
- **½ cinnamon stick**
- **½ vanilla bean**
- **11 large figs**
- **¼ cup sugar**
- **3 tablespoons unsalted butter**

The fig is not an easy fruit to enjoy. Its consistency is quite weird. My sister used to be scared by its flesh. During my time with Alain Ducasse, I realized that the fig can be a top-quality ingredient and can be present on a 3-Michelin-star menu. I really respect this fruit; it is the symbol of what summer has left behind—a lot of sun transformed into sugar through the fruit.

In a large pot combine the red wine, sugar, orange, lemon, cinnamon, and vanilla bean. Bring to a boil.

When it is boiling, add the figs, remove from the heat, and let them marinate until the sangria cools.

Into a little saucepan, put the sugar and butter. Slowly heat it and wait until it caramelizes. Add the figs and roll them in the caramel very slowly for less than a minute.

Cut the figs in half, put them in a soup plate, and cover with the sangria.

You can eat this warm or cold.

COMPOTE OF FIGS & ALMOND

Difficulty level: medium
Calories: 150
Preparation time: 2 hours 20 minutes

Serves 4

As many late-season figs as you can find

Ground almonds (a third of the volume of the figs)

Superfine sugar (a third of the volume of the figs, and extra for frying the bread)

Water (a third of the volume of the figs)

Some thick slices of rustic French bread

2 tablespoons unsalted butter

Put the figs into a large pan on a low heat and smash them with a wooden spoon. Add the ground almonds and continue stirring. Pour in the sugar and the water. Cover and let them cook at a very slow simmer.

Make sure that the mixture cooks very slowly and that it doesn't burn at the bottom of the pan. After 2 hours of cooking, remove the cover and evaporate the water that may be left on top.

Cut the bread into thick finger shapes. In a pan, add a teaspoon of butter and sugar. When the butter starts turning brown, add the bread to the pan and cook on both sides until it turns golden brown.

Cover the bread with the fig jam. You can also add some honey, yogurt, or crème fraîche.

The compote can be frozen for future use or kept in the fridge for no more than 5 days.

GRAPE

The grape is one of the oldest known cultivated fruits. It is grown for wine making and for the table. Its color starts from palest green up to dark ruby red. I have always been a grape fan. Its taste has always appealed to me as far back as I can remember. I am actually quite sad not to remember the day I fell in love with grapes. How old was I? Who made me eat my first grape? No idea. My memory cannot go as far back as I would like sometimes. So I spend most years refusing to eat grapes until I can get hold of the first grape of the season in mid-August. It is such a reward for me. I am always so proud not to have bastardized my love for grapes with something from the other side of the world: a seedless little bowl of sugar that does not remotely taste of real grape. When I see my kids raving about their grapes in February, I just want to cry. Seriously!

FRESH GRAPES (IN SEASON)

Difficulty level: easy

Serves 1

Grapes

Remember that the best way to appreciate grapes is to eat them on their own. With nothing else!

Make sure you know the kind of grape that you love and just indulge.

SAUTÉED GRAPES & ELDERFLOWER *(Pictured)*

Difficulty level: medium
Calories: 110
Preparation time: 50 minutes

Serves 4

1 tablespoon unsalted butter

14 oz. slightly off & starting to get soft grapes (washed & removed from their stalks)

½ cup white wine (Sauvignon Blanc)

1 tablespoon elderflower cordial

1 handful elderflower flowers

When the grapes are going slightly off, it is time to do something with them. This recipe brings together two ingredients that complement each other very well. The oversweetness of an old grape will be balanced by the subtlety and deepness of flavor of the elderflower. It is like chewing a glass of Sauvignon Blanc!

Melt the butter in a hot pan and start tossing the grapes in it. Make sure the heat is very low and gentle. Add the white wine and the cordial. Boil and reduce half of the liquid.

Remove from the heat and divide among 4 low tumblers and cover with the fresh elderflowers. Serve immediately.

LEMON LAYER PUDDING

Difficulty level: medium
Calories: 380
Preparation time: 1 hour

Only after spending many years wondering about the qualities of the lemon, I realized it is a very subtle fruit. A fruit that needs to be understood before being judged! A fruit that is very strong on its own and the perfect partner for many things. Chewing a lemon is a great experience: it is very acidic at the beginning but then when your tastebuds get used to it, you realize that the taste is so concentrated that it is going to stay in your mouth for ages after swallowing.

Serves 4

- ½ stick (4 tablespoons) unsalted butter
- 2 lemons (zest & juice)
- ¾ cup granulated sugar
- 2 eggs (separated)
- ¾ cup whole milk
- ½ cup self-rising flour
- Pinch of salt
- Plain probiotic yogurt (such as Activia)

My favorite is the lemon from Menton in the South of France, where they make a lemon so sweet that you can almost eat it like an apple!

Preheat the oven to 325°F.

In a bowl, whisk the butter, lemon juice, lemon zest, and sugar. Cream the mixture until it looks pale and a little fluffy. Add the egg yolks and beat well. Stir in the milk.

Fold in the flour and the salt. Whisk the egg white until stiff and fold in carefully with the other ingredients.

Pour into a buttered ovenproof dish (or a Pac-Man silicone mold, pictured). Stand the dish in a shallow tin of water and cook at the top of the oven for 40 minutes. The top of the lemon cake should be firm to the touch. Serve warm with a spoonful of yogurt.

PEPPERED LEMON INFUSION

Sugared celery & mint

Difficulty level: easy
Calories: 140
Preparation time: 1 hour

Serves 4

3 bunches celery hearts

4 cups water

1 cup superfine sugar

1 bunch lemongrass

2 gelatin sheets

4 lemons (zest & juice)

½ bunch mint

¾ oz. ground Malaysian black peppercorns

Slice the celery into long, thin strips. Keep them in ice-cold water for 10 minutes, until they become crunchy.

Boil the water with the sugar and the lemongrass. Boil for 5 minutes and let it cool down for 5 minutes.

Add the gelatin sheets and the lemon zest and let it cool down until it is at room temperature. Add the lemon juice.

Pass through a sieve and divide the infusion among 4 large bowls.

Chop the fresh mint and mix it with the celery.

Place the celery in the middle of each bowl and refrigerate until the liquid looks a little set.

Grind pepper over just before serving.

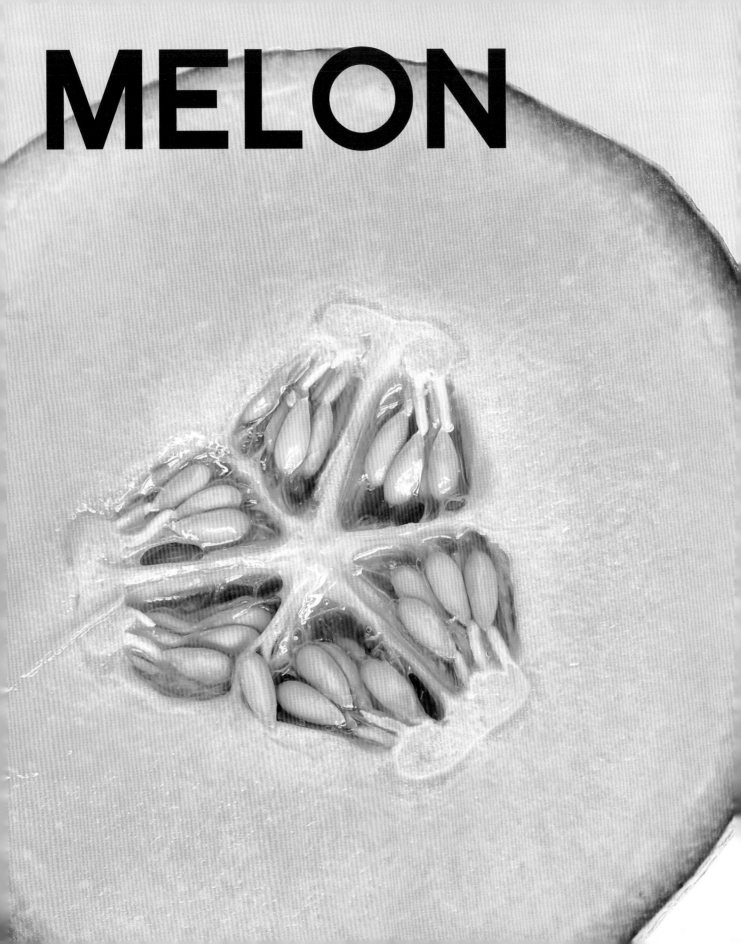

MELON

In her book *An Omelette and a Glass of Wine*, Elizabeth David tells of her experience in the Cavaillon fruit and vegetable market. She describes the early morning and the very strong smell of melon.

When I read it, I could easily smell it too: the melon gives off a very particular fragrance. During the melon season (May/June—or to early July) Cavaillon becomes its world capital. (At least that is what I thought until I discovered that there were other places in the world that grew melon!)

The Charentais or Cavaillon melon is the best type of melon and in order to recognize if it is good or not, you need to smell it *au cul* (from the ass).

When I was first told this, I didn't really understand why I should smell it from somewhere other than from my nose. I should have understood that it meant the melon *cul.* Not mine!

If it smells strong, very settled, and pure, then it is good. If it smells light, green, and slightly sharp, then you should wait. If it smells like alcohol, then it is too late. Easy, no?

If your melon is perfect, then you have made the right choice. So eat it as it is. You do not need to add anything: no Port, no Italian ham—nothing.

If your melon is too green, you should wait. Be patient, as melons always ripen with age (unlike fruit from trees, like peaches).

If your melon is too ripe, you can make a purée and serve it as a pudding or even freeze it and make a granita.

MELON SOUP & FRESH GOAT CHEESE

Difficulty level: easy
Calories: 150
Preparation time: 1 hour Resting: 3 hours

Serves 4

3 oz. fresh goat cheese

1 oz. fresh ricotta cheese

½ cup extra-virgin olive oil

Salt & pepper

1 lime (juiced)

1 overripe melon

In a bowl, mix the fresh goat cheese and ricotta with the olive oil and the pepper. You need to turn them into a thick paste. Add the juice of 1 lime and add a little bit of salt. Taste and refrigerate.

Cut the melon in 2 and remove all the seeds and small threads attached to it. Spoon out the flesh into the bowl of a blender. Blend quickly until all the lumps have disappeared. Do not blend too much, as this will make the soup turn brown. Transfer the soup into a bowl and refrigerate for at least 3 hours before serving.

Make some small quenelles with the goat-cheese mix and divide them among 4 soup plates. Serve the melon soup around them. Add pepper at the end and serve.

MELON GRANITA, MINT PURÉE & SOFT TOFU

Difficulty level: medium
Calories: 80
Preparation time: 1 hour 30 minutes Resting: 2 hours

Serves 4

1 large overripe melon

½ bunch fresh mint

1 lemon (zest)

2½ oz. silken tofu

Cut the melon in 2 and remove all the seeds and threads attached to it. Spoon out the flesh into the bowl of a blender. Blend quickly until all the lumps have disappeared. Do not blend too much, as this will make the mixture turn brown.

Transfer it to a deep, flat baking sheet and freeze. Scratch the surface of the frozen melon purée every 2 to 3 hours until it turns into a granita.

Clean the blender and mix the mint leaves and the lemon zest. Slice the tofu into ⅛-inch pieces. Divide the slices among 4 soup plates.

Cover with the granita and pour the mint purée over it.

ORANGE MARMALADE

Difficulty level: easy
Calories: 45 per spoon
Preparation time: 1 hour

My great-grandmother used to tell me that she would get only two oranges for Christmas as her present. And then she found it thrilling to be able to eat the oranges! The orange is now very commonly used and consumed. It is rich in vitamin C and is indispensable for our immune systems. When the orange is brightly colored, it means that it is very rich in carotene, which is very good for fighting cancer and aging. The more acidic the orange, the better it is for a good balance of our metabolism.

Makes 20 spoonfuls

- 7 tablespoons unsalted butter
- 1¾ cups granulated sugar
- 20 oranges (washed & roughly chopped into smallish cubes)
- 1 cup water

The orange is rich in pectin and can help reduce your cholesterol. A good orange is only 74 calories: that is about the same as a container of low-fat yogurt.

The problem with oranges these days is that they are sprayed far too much with pesticides and you really need to wash them before eating. I have recently started to use a natural product called Veggi Wash, which claims to remove pesticides from fruits and vegetables. I am still alive, so . . .

In a large pot, put the butter and sugar on a high heat.

When the sugar starts turning brown, add the chopped oranges, reduce the heat, and stir for 5 minutes. Add the water, cover, and cook until ready (this usually takes 45 minutes).

You may have to add a bit of water from time to time.

The best way to eat orange marmalade is with freshly toasted sourdough bread and whipped cream.

ORANGE, TOFU & YUZU CURD

Difficulty level: hard
Calories: 140
Preparation time: 1 hour

Serves 4

4 large oranges

Pinch salt

1 lime (juiced)

2 tablespoons unsalted butter

2 tablespoons all-purpose flour

2 gelatin sheets

9 oz. soft tofu

4 large green shiso leaves (cleaned & thinly chopped)

¾ cup yuzu

Pepper

Cut the tops off the oranges and remove their flesh delicately, making sure not to break the peel.

Clean the orange peel "shells" and keep in the freezer to stabilize their color.

Pour the flesh into a blender and mix it very quickly with the salt and the lime juice. Do not overblend the orange, as you want to keep a little bit of substance to it.

In a warm pan on the stove, melt the butter with the flour until it starts drying out and looking bubbly. Pour in the orange pulp and stir for 3 minutes. Bring it to a boil and transfer the contents of the pan to another bowl, add the gelatin sheets, stir, and leave to cool.

When cooled, add the tofu and mix with a fork. Add the chopped shiso leaves and the yuzu.

Take the orange shells out of the freezer and fill them with the mixture.

Add some freshly ground black pepper and serve.

Note: Yuzu is a citrus fruit mainly used in Japanese cooking and tastes like a combination of grapefruit, sweet orange, and lemon.

Green shiso is a bit citrusy, with a hint of basil.

ORANGE BLOSSOM MARSHMALLOW

Difficulty level: hard
Calories: 90
Preparation time: 1 hour Setting time: 2 hours

Serves 4

2 cups water

2 oz. gelatin sheets

1 tablespoon lemon juice

1 cup orange blossom water

1⅔ cups corn syrup

2⅔ cups confectioners' sugar

Cornstarch mixed with confectioners' sugar for dusting

Divide the water in 2. Boil in 2 pans. Remove one from the heat and dissolve the gelatin and transfer to a mixing bowl. Add the lemon juice and the orange blossom water.

Add the corn syrup and sugar to the other pot of boiling water and bring the mixture to 240°F.

When the temperature is reached, slowly pour the hot sugar solution in a thin stream into the gelatin solution, beating all the time. Continue to beat until the maximum volume is reached (about 5 minutes).

Pour the mixture into a baking sheet dusted with confectioners' sugar and cornstarch. Leave to set for 2 hours.

When set, cut into cubes and dust the pieces in a mixture of confectioners' sugar and cornstarch.

PEACH

If there was one fruit I could describe as the King of Summer Fruit, it would be the peach. The peach is seasonally right. I mean that when the peach is ready to be eaten is when you need it the most.

During my childhood, I knew that after the strawberries, the peaches would come and this would mean eating outside almost every night in the garden with my parents. Hot days and warm evenings in the South of France.

What I needed then to rehydrate my body was something juicy and slightly sweet, easy to eat, and affordable. The peach was the answer. And I was very lucky to be able to help myself directly from the trees—which did not actually belong to me or my parents.

So I got caught helping myself!

A farmer, who didn't really like the idea of me eating his peaches, caught me red-handed (well, light pink-handed actually). He should have been so grateful that I was eating only the perfectly ripened ones, the juiciest ones—it was a sign of me recognizing the great job he had done on his peaches. He didn't! He chased me and caught me and made sure that I would never do it again. I was so frightened. I never did it again.

The peach is originally from China, but was brought to Europe by the Persians. Louis XIV was a peach lover and gave the name to his favorite *Téton de Venus* or *Venus nipples* (I like those kitschy names; French kings sometimes had a lot of finesse).

My favorite has always been the vine peach, or *pêche de vigne*. This type is the tastiest and my grandmother wouldn't eat any other peach but this one.

I was very lucky to be able to eat those little peaches because it is very hard to find them. The white peach (its near cousin) is almost as good and is easier to find in July and August at a supermarket.

I have seen people not touching, feeling, or smelling their peaches before buying them. I wonder how they eat them. Do they eat them like an apple? I mean crunchy? I hope not! Supermarkets should employ peach choosers in season to guide people how to make their choices. I am sure that we would consume more peaches.

The peach is also lucky to be one of the healthiest fruits around. Very low in calories, rich in fiber and potassium, and good for balancing your metabolism.

3 SIMPLE WAYS TO EAT PEACHES

Difficulty level: easy
Calories: 150
Preparation time: 3 hours 30 minutes

UNDERRIPE PEACHES

Serves 4

4 unripe peaches

½ cup extra-virgin olive oil

¼ teaspoon salt

2 tablespoons granulated sugar

¼ teaspoon pepper

8 raw shrimp

Pat unsalted butter

3 tablespoons sherry vinegar

¼ cup shrimp jus (see page 31)

Semi-dried peaches, shrimp & sherry vinegar

Cut the peaches into quarters and put them on a plate with olive oil, salt, sugar, and pepper. Put them in a very low temperature oven (200°F) for 3 hours, until they are semi-dry while retaining a bit of moisture.

In a hot pan, add a spoonful of olive oil. When the oil starts smoking, add the shrimp and cook them for 1 minute on each side. Lower the heat and add the butter. Toss the shrimp and remove them. Put the pan back on the heat and add the vinegar and the shrimp jus. Reduce a little and pour over the shrimp.

You can add them to a green leaf salad or pair with a grilled fish. The peach taste will concentrate during the cooking process and will bring another dimension to the fish.

PEFECTLY RIPE PEACHES

Calories: 000
Preparation time: 0 minutes

Nothing much to do! Quickly wash the peach under room-temperature water.

Bite into the peach and let the juice slightly drip off your mouth—as if you were drinking some . . . well, I can't think of anything to add! I like the feeling of the warm, tender, cat-tongue-like peach skin that explodes under the pressure of my teeth and releases the cold juice in my mouth.

So sexy!

OVERRIPE PEACHES

Calories: 95
Preparation time: 5 minutes

Serves 1

Prosecco

1 peach

Don't worry, it is the best reason to prepare the famous Bellini cocktail. First, explode the peach in your hand over a large glass. Rinse your hand with Prosecco over the glass.

Stir a bit and drink very cold.

PEAR

My earliest memory of a pear was the sight of one sitting in a thin clear bottle in the cabinet we used to have in my parents' dining room. Funnily enough, I never thought then that it could have been the same fruit as the one I loved in purée when I was very young.

My parents adored pear alcohol. There wasn't a family dinner not finished by a few small glasses of pear—*La Poire,* it was called. They were all so high by the end of a meal that La Poire sounded like a medicinal drink.

It was good for everything: not putting on weight, better digestion, relaxation, headaches, tummy aches . . . And I am sure that to them it was also good for reducing the hole in the ozone layer, peace on earth, and France winning the next football World Cup . . . La Poire was a must!

I am not a big fan of La Poire. I much prefer the original fruit, especially the English Comice pear. It comes slightly later in the pear season, around the beginning of autumn.

Like Bosc pears, Comice have meaty flesh and are still firm when fully ripe. The French would tell you that Bosc are better because the Comice stay on the tree too long due to of the awful English weather. They never seem to ripen. And I would say that it is exactly the reason why they are so superior!

As with strawberries, English pears are a lot tastier and less sugary than the ones from France.

The Comice is ideal for poaching because it resists turning to mush when cooked. On top of that it has the advantage of keeping its skin smooth, and it does not crack.

POACHED AND CARAMELIZED COMICE PEARS

Difficulty level: medium
Calories: 180
Preparation time: 45 minutes

Serves 4

- ¼ cup superfine sugar
- ¾ cup water
- 1 lemon (juiced)
- ¾ cup red cooking wine
- 8 Comice pears (peeled & left whole)
- 1 spoonful dark molasses
- 2 tablespoons balsamic vinegar

Put the sugar in a large saucepan together with the water.

Put on a low heat and cook until the sugar turns to caramel. Add the lemon juice and the wine. Remove from the heat and place the pears in the pan. Add the molasses and the balsamic vinegar and cover.

Cook for 20 minutes at a low heat.

Serve the pears at room temperature covered in their own cooking syrup.

POACHED WILLIAMS PEAR & CHOCOLATE TART

Difficulty level: hard
Calories: 350 (for 2 helpings)
Preparation time: 5 hours

Serves 4

Tart base

- 1¼ cups all-purpose flour
- 1 tablespoon superfine sugar
- 1½ teaspoons salt
- 9 tablespoons unsalted butter (cut into big squares at room temperature, softened)
- 1 egg
- 1 tablespoon water

Pears

- 8 Williams pears (peeled & cored)
- 1 cup superfine sugar
- 6 cups water
- ½ vanilla bean (cut in 2)

Chocolate filling

- 4 eggs
- 9 oz. ground almonds
- ¾ cup heavy cream
- ½ cup low-fat milk
- Pinch salt
- ½ cup dark cocoa powder

Making the tart base

In a bowl, mix the flour, sugar, salt, and the butter with your hands until you get a crumbly texture. Break in the egg and add the spoonful of water. Continue working the mix until it comes together as a fragile dough.

Remove the dough from the bowl and continue working it in your hands on a clean, floured surface. Do not overwork the dough, as it is always better when it is a little crumbled rather than tense and elastic.

Cover with plastic wrap and keep in the fridge for at least 4 hours before using.

Poaching the pears

Place the pears in a deep, heavy-bottomed pan. Add sugar, water, and the vanilla bean. Slowly boil for 15 minutes. Let the pears cool in the cooking syrup.

When cooled, cut them into four and dry them on a clean dish towel.

Making the chocolate filling

In a bowl, whisk the eggs together with the ground almonds. Add the cream and the milk. Add the salt and cocoa powder.

Finishing the tart

Preheat the oven to 350°F. Roll out the dough and place in a buttered 12-inch tart pan. Place the pears on the pastry and cover them with the cocoa and almond mix.

Cook in the oven for 25 minutes.

Serve warm.

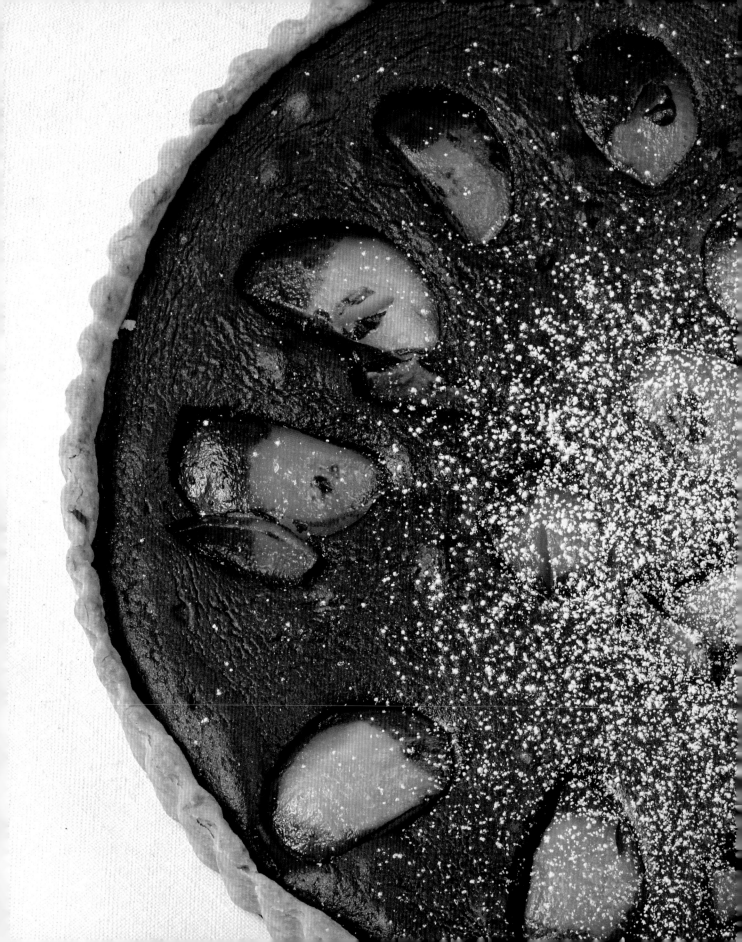

PLUM

The plum is an aristocratic family of fruits. Not many other fruits have so many cousins: different sizes, colors, textures. You have the small purple ones; the large, thin- or thick-skinned ones; the yellow furry-textured one; the glutinous, almost black ones; and many other types coming from almost all parts of the world. As a cook, it is one of those ingredients with which your imagination can really go wild when you start creating with it. Raw, roasted, pulped, or frozen—plums can take almost any treatment and will always end up tasting delicious.

A COOKED RED PLUM *(Pictured)*

Difficulty level: medium
Calories: 120
Preparation time: 30 minutes

Serves 4

- 1 red plum per person
- 2 teaspoons of honey per plum
- ½ teaspoon cumin seeds
- 1 teaspoon Cognac per plum

Wash and dry the plums, put them on a baking sheet, and pour the honey over them.

Add the cumin seeds and the Cognac and put in the oven at 325°F for 20 minutes.

They can be served on their own or with a dollop of Greek yogurt.

A RIPE PLUM

Difficulty level: easy
Calories: 120

Serves 1

- 1 Santa Rosa plum

If there is one type of plum that should be eaten when ripe and therefore soft, it is the Santa Rosa. Early Santa Rosa season plums do not have a strong plum taste. They can actually sometimes be a bit watery.

The end-of-season ones have taken the sun a lot more and have had time to diffuse their taste from the stone to the flesh. The taste is deep and complicated.

Its skin can be a little bit astringent but behind it is a sweet and thick juice. The longer you wait, the better it becomes.

CARAMELIZED GREENGAGE & PASTIS

Fresh goat cheese

Difficulty level: medium
Calories: 280
Preparation time: 45 minutes

The English greengage (or *Reine Claude* in French) is a complicated end-of-summer/early-autumn fruit. Where I come from, we would soak them in alcohol—then drink the alcohol and throw away the fruits. But that is because I am French! Here, once again, caramelizing the fruit is best in order to concentrate the taste and remove a bit of the acidity.

Serves 4

- 9 oz. greengages (halved, pits removed)
- 3 tablespoons unsalted butter
- ¾ oz. ground almonds
- ⅓ cup brown sugar
- ¼ cup Pastis
- 2½ oz. fresh goat cheese
- ¾ oz. sliced almonds

Rinse the cut greengages under cold water. Add the butter to a hot pan and when it turns brown, add the greengages, ground almonds, and brown sugar and roast for 3 minutes.

Cover and continue cooking for an extra 2 minutes, making sure that they don't dry out. Add the Pastis and flambé while stirring the pan so the plums get coated with the Pastis flavor.

Cut some slices of goat cheese and sandwich them between the halves of greengage, making them look like green burgers, and sprinkle over some sliced almonds. Finish them in the oven (broil position) for 2 minutes.

PERSIMMON

Difficulty level: easy
Calories: 47 (for 1½ oz. fruit)
Preparation time: as long you like

There are a few things that remind me of autumn, but the sight of a persimmon tree with its fruit clinging is really characteristic of the season. The South of France is very rich in persimmon trees, especially Avignon and its region. I remember the first time I had a ripe persimmon like it was yesterday. My mother said it would be like eating an oyster. It was like a slippery jelly that lingered in my mouth. It was beautiful.

The texture of the persimmon doesn't enter my mouth as often as I would like and I would not offer a persimmon to someone I don't know; otherwise they might think I am a very kinky person!

Some varieties of persimmon can be eaten while still hard, but the sensations are completely different and it becomes very boring.

I like the Hachiya, a big persimmon that requires full ripening. I like the fact that you have to wait in order to eat it. The fact that you have to touch it every day, sometimes for weeks, before it is ready is super exciting for me. The more you wait, the more precious it becomes.

I would like to have customers who would come every day and ask me whether the persimmons were ripe or not. If not, they would say, "Okay, I'll come back tomorrow, and the day after and the day after until the fruit is ready!"

You know the persimmon is ready if when you cut it, a soft and translucent pulp is revealed all the way to the center of the fruit. Plant a spoon in it and eat slowly. Chew as much as you can and try to savor the experience for as long as possible.

FLAMING PERSIMMON WITH CALVADOS

Difficulty level: easy
Calories: 120
Preparation time: 10 minutes

Serves 4

¾ cup heavy cream

1 tablespoon confectioners' sugar

4 persimmon (perfectly soft, ready to explode)

½ cup Calvados

Whisk the cream in a cold bowl until it starts to firm. Add the confectioners' sugar and whisk one last time to set the cream.

Choose the best persimmon available. When perfectly ripe, remove the skin on the top of the fruit and put it on a serving plate.

In a small pan, slowly heat up the Calvados, making sure not to boil it.

When hot, pour over the persimmon and flambé it.

Serve the cream on the side.

SUGARED QUINCE *Carrot & olive oil*

Difficulty level: hard
Calories: 75
Preparation time: 4 hours

British quinces are certainly the best fruit grown on the island and are perhaps the most unknown and unused. Unripe quinces are unpalatable—their flesh is astringent—but when ripe, their yellow skin has a fragrance similar to pineapple. Quince is the best thing to eat between meals. Classy snack! This amazing taste is somehow lost in cooking. I don't know why the tradition wants us to cook the quince. When ripe, it is the perfect fruit.

Serves 8

- 3 tablespoons unsalted butter
- 2 quinces (peeled, cored & roughly cut into large cubes)
- 2 large carrots (peeled & thickly chopped)
- ⅔ cup brown sugar
- ½ cup extra-virgin olive oil
- 1 cup water
- ½ cup superfine sugar

A quince is very low in calories (30 calories per 3 ounces) compared to the pear (50 calories per 3 ounces), and it is not very high in sugar (7g compared to 12g for pear). I usually suggest that you eat this fruit raw and very ripe. You do not need a recipe for that!

However, when cooked, the quince is a wonderful vehicle for other flavors to shine. In the restaurant, we found that quince can be very good when served with bergamot oil and carrot leaves. It is also great when mixed with spices—it tends to soften their power.

Into a hot saucepan, add the butter, and when it starts foaming, add the quince, carrot, brown sugar, olive oil, and water. Cover and cook at a very low heat for 2 hours.

Make sure that you don't overstir during the cooking process, otherwise it will remove some of the taste of the fruit (it sounds weird, but it is the surprising conclusion I came to wondering for many years why it sometimes didn't taste the same).

Once cooked, blitz in a mixer and pour onto an oiled baking sheet. Cover with plastic wrap and put in the fridge for at least 4 hours so it has time to set.

Once set, cut into large cubes and cover them with sugar.

You can store in the fridge for up to 6 days.

WINTER SPICED QUINCE

Crispy pancetta & black pepper

Difficulty level: medium
Calories: 200
Preparation time: 3 hours

Serves 4

1 teaspoon clear honey

⅔ cup brown sugar

3 cups water

4 quinces (peeled, cored & quartered)

½ vanilla bean, split lengthwise

1 teaspoon ground cinnamon

1 lemon (zest)

4 whole cloves

8 thin pancetta slices

Pepper

In a heavy saucepan, dissolve the honey, brown sugar, and water. Add the quinces, vanilla bean, cinnamon, the lemon zest, and the cloves. Bring to a slow simmer and cook for at least 2 hours with a cover.

Pan-fry the slices of pancetta until crispy and rest them on a clean dish towel/paper towels to remove the excess fat.

On a large plate, place the quinces and the crispy pancetta slices.

Add some freshly ground pepper just before serving.

WHAT TO DO WHEN THE QUINCE NEVER SEEMS TO RIPEN?

The quince for those who like to wait . . .

You need to buy a very hard quince early in the season. Surround it with some red apples and wait! Wait until the quince becomes softer. Turn it by a quarter every day and wait. You may have to wait for weeks. But when the quince is perfectly ripe, the experience is well worth the wait!

RHUBARB

We, the French, don't understand anything about rhubarb, nor do we know anything about it. I had never seen or heard of rhubarb until the age of 20. So the day I was faced with my first rhubarb, my reaction was, What the hell is this watery, half-finished red celery?

It looked weird and uninspiring for a closed-minded young French chef like me. Seriously, if I was meant to cook this plant, surely Escoffier would have listed it in his *Guide Culinaire*. I looked up my chef's bible and there was nothing starting with the letters "Rhu" in the index.

Then, when I asked if it was a vegetable or a fruit, nobody really knew about that either. Sorry, but we French don't cook hermaphrodite plants—you are either a vegetable or a fruit.

That was almost 20 years ago and it is time that I apologized for my original treatment of rhubarb. Sorry for having been brought up as a closed-minded, ego-inflated, better-than-anybody, young French chef twat.

Sorry. Sorry. Sorry.

I have learned to understand the complexity of rhubarb and have created a seriously stunning combination of rhubarb, lemon, and pepper that I sometimes serve with fresh goat cheese.

COMPOTE OF RHUBARB

Indonesian long peppercorns & fresh goat cheese

Difficulty level: easy
Calories: 220
Preparation time: 1 hour Resting: 12 hours

Serves 4

1 lemon skin

2 teaspoons Indonesian long peppercorns

2 tablespoons unsalted butter

10 oz. rhubarb (peeled & cut in 1-inch-thick pieces)

⅓ cup superfine sugar

½ cup water

2½ oz. fresh goat cheese

Pepper

Cut a 4-inch x 4-inch piece of cheesecloth. Put the lemon skin and the Indonesian long peppercorns in the middle. Close it and tie firmly.

In a hot, thick-bottomed pan, melt the butter until it turns foamy. Pour the rhubarb in and stir gently, making sure that it does not brown.

Add the sugar and continue stirring for at least 2 minutes, making sure that the sugar has dissolved. Add the lemon, pepper bag, and the water.

Bring to a boil and slowly cook at a very low heat. The rhubarb will start losing its water, so you should never cover this compote with a lid. After 7 minutes, the rhubarb will have started to look less watery and more like a compote texture. Remove from the heat and let it cool down.

Transfer into a bowl, cover tightly with plastic wrap, and keep it in the fridge for at least 12 hours.

Divide the goat cheese among 4 small bowls. Remove the lemon and spice bag from the rhubarb compote and serve the compote on top of the fresh cheese. You can add a spoonful of sugar on top of each plate and a little freshly ground pepper.

STRAWBERRY

The strawberry is the number-one fruit for those who want to lose weight and, together with the kiwi, the richest in vitamin C. The only problem is that it is getting more and more difficult to find good strawberries.

Strawberries are victims of their own success. Everyone loves them and producers and supermarkets now manage to sell them all year long. I can't really think of any other fruit that is so delicious during its natural season and so disgusting outside it.

A freshly picked strawberry, not overrefrigerated and with a thin skin that looks like it is going to explode, always gives off a very delicate aroma. It is subtle and refined and the aroma lingers in your mouth for minutes after you swallow.

They are so unlike out-of-season strawberries, which taste watery and over-refrigerated and have no particular flavor or depth. They also have a much tougher skin and are quite often not as sugary as the ones you would buy during their natural season.

The strawberry has become a symbol of the "you want it, you have it" society we live in. It is sad but I am certain that the more refined about our taste we become, the more we should just refuse to buy out-of-season produce and wait for the best local strawberries to be in season.

Patience and evolution are key.

STRAWBERRIES

Granita, sautéed & in their own juice

During the season, I usually find strawberries in three stages: underripe, overripe, and ripe. These are the best way to eat this fruit under many forms and textures.

UNDERRIPE STRAWBERRIES

Difficulty level: easy
Calories: 135
Preparation time: 10 minutes

Serves 4

1 lb. 4 oz. underripe strawberries, destemmed

2 tablespoons unsalted butter

⅓ cup superfine sugar

Rinse them and dry the berries very well. Put a saucepan on the heat. When hot, add butter. When the butter turns brown, throw in 1 spoonful of sugar and the strawberries. Sauté for 1 minute and serve immediately.

PERFECTLY RIPE STRAWBERRIES

Difficulty level: medium
Calories: 160
Preparation time: 7 hours

Serves 4

1 lb. 4 oz. overripe strawberries, destemmed

1 cup water

½ cup granulated sugar

Cut the strawberries into quarters and put them in a bowl with the water and the sugar.

Gently toss them and put them in the fridge and wait at least 6 hours before eating.

OVERRIPE STRAWBERRIES

Difficulty level: medium
Calories: 180
Preparation time: 12 hours

Serves 4

1 lb. 4 oz. overripe strawberries, destemmed

½ cup superfine sugar

½ cup water

Blend the strawberries together with the water and sugar. Transfer them to the freezer in flat containers. Leave to set for 2 hours.

Scratch the surface of the liquid with a fork every hour to get a granita texture.

INDEX

www.crownpublishing.com
www.clarksonpotter.com

CLARKSON POTTER is a trademark and POTTER with
colophon is a registered trademark of Random House, Inc.

This edition published by arrangement with Preface
Publishing, an imprint of The Random House Group
Limited, London.

Library of Congress Cataloging-in-Publication Data

Gauthier, Alexis
  Vegetronic / Alexis Gauthier ; photographs by James
Lewis. -- First American edition.
     pages cm
  Includes index.

  1. Cooking (Vegetables) I. Title.

  TX801.G385 2013
  641.6'5--dc23

                         2013015323

Printed in China

Cover design by Olga Grlic
Cover photographs © 2013 Johnny & Mary

10 9 8 7 6 5 4 3 2 1

First American Edition